ANIMALS
on the Inside

Contents

Translation by Betty Welker

Edited by Dr. Nancy B. Simmons, Assistant Curator,
Department of Mammalogy, American Museum
of Natural History

10 9 8 7 6 5 4 3 2 1

Published 1994 by Sterling Publishing Company, Inc.
387 Park Avenue South, New York, N.Y. 10016
Originally published in Spain by Planeta DeAgostini
under the title *El Libro de los Animales por Dentro*
© 1994 by Ediciones Este, S.A.
English translation © 1994 Sterling Publishing Co., Inc.
Distributed in Canada by Sterling Publishing
% Canadian Manda Group, P.O. Box 920, Station U
Toronto, Ontario, Canada M8Z 5P9
Distributed in Great Britain and Europe by Cassell PLC
Villiers House, 41/47 Strand, London WC2N 5JE, England
Distributed in Australia by Capricorn Link (Australia) Pty Ltd.
P.O. Box 6651, Baulkham Hills, Business Centre, NSW 2153, Australia
Printed and bound in Spain
All rights reserved

Sterling   ISBN 0-8069-0830-0

Library of Congress Cataloging-in-Publication Data
Llamas Ruiz, Andrés.
    [Libro de los animales por dentro. English]
    Animals on the inside / Andrés Llamas Ruiz ; [translation by Betty
Welker].
        p.   cm.
    Includes index.
    ISBN 0-8069-0830-0
    1. Anatomy—Juvenile literature.   2. Animals—Juvenile literature.
[1. Anatomy. 2. Animals.] I. Title.
QL806.5.L5813 1994
591.4—dc20
                                                                94-17467
                                                                CIP
                                                                AC

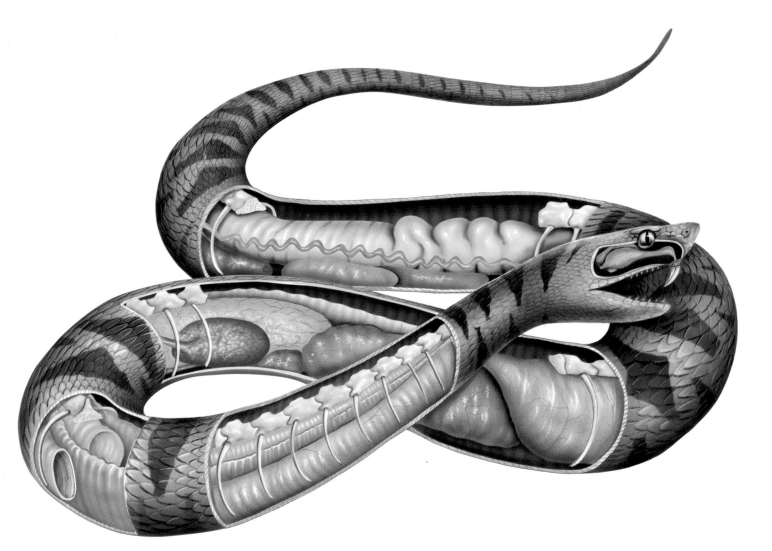

ANIMALS
on the Inside

A BOOK OF DISCOVERY & LEARNING

ANDRES LLAMAS RUIZ

 Sterling Publishing Co., Inc. New York

Insects and spiders

Almost a million species of insects are known, and new ones are continually being discovered. Insects have six legs, a body divided into three segments protected by an outer covering—the exoskeleton—and most have wings. The insect group includes species as different as the butterfly, the beetle and the ant. Spiders are not insects. They have eight legs and no wings.

Bees, like wasps and ants, belong to the order *Hymenoptera*.

A well-organized community.

Most bees are solitary insects. Some females even abandon their eggs after laying them. Honeybees live in colonies of thousands, and share work and food. In a hive, there are from 30,000 to 60,000 workers performing different jobs, depending on their ages; 100 to 200 drones, idle male bees whose only function is to fertilize the queen bee; and the queen bee herself, whose only job is to lay eggs.

A honey factory. Flowers produce a sweet liquid called nectar that worker bees like very much. They suck it in, and fly back to the hive. When they get there, they feed the nectar to other workers, who swallow it and mix it with their own saliva. Later they regurgitate it and deposit it in small open cells in the hive, where it dries up. The liquid thickens and becomes honey.

Dance of the bees. When they find flowers rich in nectar, the bees return to the hive and "tell" the other bees by doing a dance. If the flowers are close by—less than 82 feet (25m) away, they do a "round" dance. When flowers are farther away, they do a "waggle" dance that makes their middles shake, and signals the direction of the flowers.

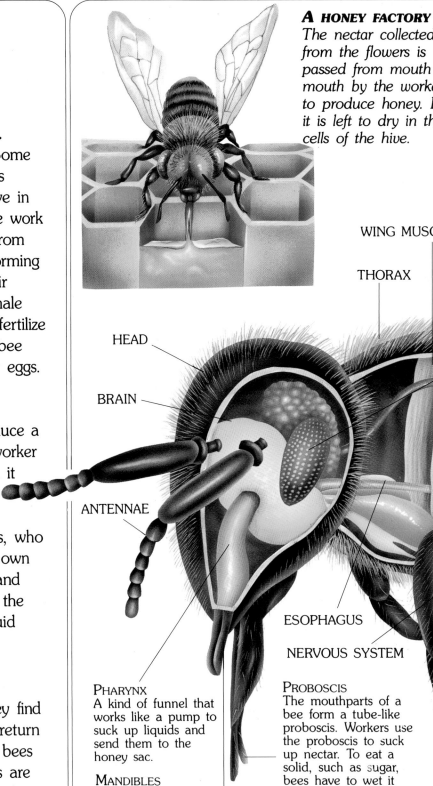

A HONEY FACTORY
The nectar collected from the flowers is passed from mouth to mouth by the workers to produce honey. Later it is left to dry in the cells of the hive.

WING MUSCLES

THORAX

HEAD

BRAIN

ANTENNAE

ESOPHAGUS

NERVOUS SYSTEM

PHARYNX
A kind of funnel that works like a pump to suck up liquids and send them to the honey sac.

MANDIBLES
These two jaw-like pieces work at the same time, the way scissors do. Bees use them to cut and shape the wax, open pollen sacs of flowers, collect pollen, and gather dead larvae and dirt from the hive.

PROBOSCIS
The mouthparts of a bee form a tube-like proboscis. Workers use the proboscis to suck up nectar. To eat a solid, such as sugar, bees have to wet it first with saliva so that they can suck it up. The proboscis of a queen or drone is much shorter than that of a worker bee.

10

THE BEE: A VERY SWEET LIFE

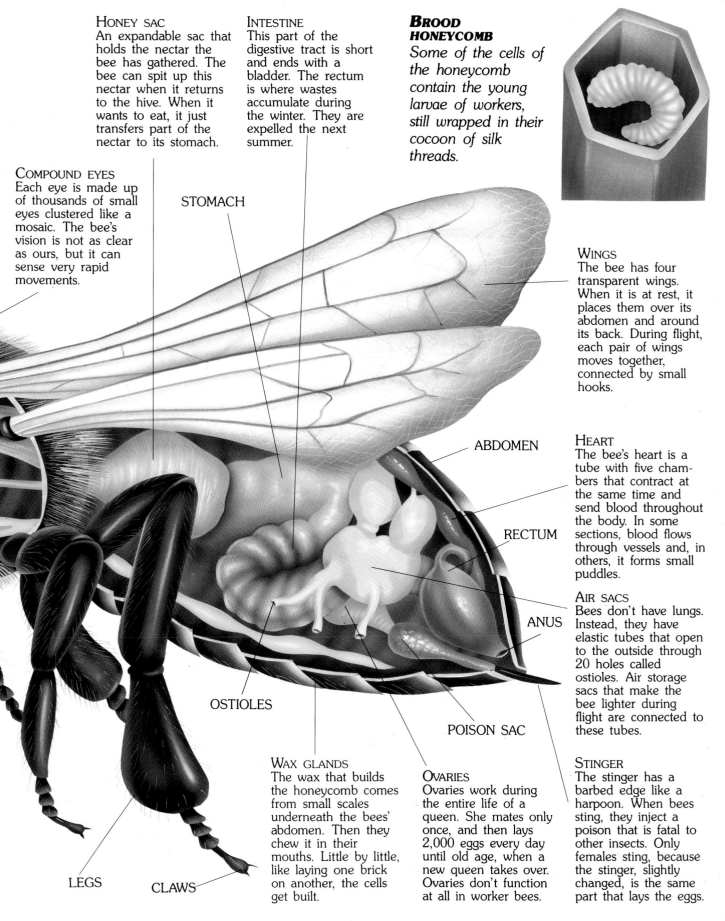

HONEY SAC
An expandable sac that holds the nectar the bee has gathered. The bee can spit up this nectar when it returns to the hive. When it wants to eat, it just transfers part of the nectar to its stomach.

INTESTINE
This part of the digestive tract is short and ends with a bladder. The rectum is where wastes accumulate during the winter. They are expelled the next summer.

BROOD HONEYCOMB
Some of the cells of the honeycomb contain the young larvae of workers, still wrapped in their cocoon of silk threads.

COMPOUND EYES
Each eye is made up of thousands of small eyes clustered like a mosaic. The bee's vision is not as clear as ours, but it can sense very rapid movements.

STOMACH

WINGS
The bee has four transparent wings. When it is at rest, it places them over its abdomen and around its back. During flight, each pair of wings moves together, connected by small hooks.

ABDOMEN

HEART
The bee's heart is a tube with five chambers that contract at the same time and send blood throughout the body. In some sections, blood flows through vessels and, in others, it forms small puddles.

RECTUM

AIR SACS
Bees don't have lungs. Instead, they have elastic tubes that open to the outside through 20 holes called ostioles. Air storage sacs that make the bee lighter during flight are connected to these tubes.

ANUS

OSTIOLES

POISON SAC

WAX GLANDS
The wax that builds the honeycomb comes from small scales underneath the bees' abdomen. Then they chew it in their mouths. Little by little, like laying one brick on another, the cells get built.

OVARIES
Ovaries work during the entire life of a queen. She mates only once, and then lays 2,000 eggs every day until old age, when a new queen takes over. Ovaries don't function at all in worker bees.

STINGER
The stinger has a barbed edge like a harpoon. When bees sting, they inject a poison that is fatal to other insects. Only females sting, because the stinger, slightly changed, is the same part that lays the eggs.

LEGS

CLAWS

THE BUTTERFLY:

Butterflies belong to the order *Lepidoptera*. These beautiful insects live all over the world, but don't look for them at the North or South Pole or mountains with permanent snowcaps.

A four-part life. Butterflies look completely different at each stage of their lives. This is because of an exciting process called "metamorphosis." A few days after the female lays her eggs, hungry caterpillars hatch from them. They eat leaves, and as they grow, they shed their skins many times for roomier ones. After the last skin is shed, the caterpillar moves on to the next phase and makes a chrysalis, or cocoon. In this stage, the caterpillar is called a pupa. It is wrapped like a mummy inside a cocoon of silk, and great changes take place. At last, the adult butterfly breaks open the chrysalis and, unfolding its wings, flies away.

Defensive strategies. As caterpillars, pupas and adults, butterflies have different ways of defending themselves. When they are caterpillars, their body hair is sometimes prickly and causes itching. They also strike menacing poses to discourage their enemies. During the chrysalis phase, they are generally safe, since they are either buried in trees or hung from them. As adults, they camouflage themselves, using colors to warn their enemies that they are poisonous—or if they're not, to pretend that they are.

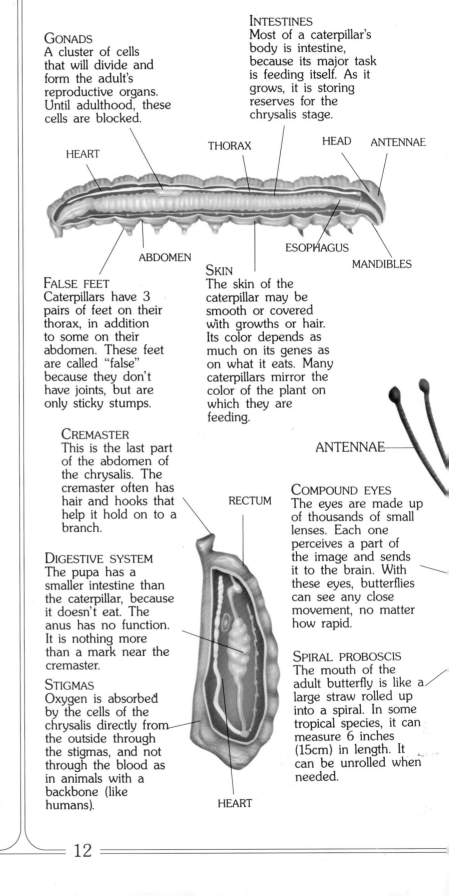

GONADS
A cluster of cells that will divide and form the adult's reproductive organs. Until adulthood, these cells are blocked.

INTESTINES
Most of a caterpillar's body is intestine, because its major task is feeding itself. As it grows, it is storing reserves for the chrysalis stage.

HEART

THORAX

HEAD   ANTENNAE

ABDOMEN

ESOPHAGUS

MANDIBLES

FALSE FEET
Caterpillars have 3 pairs of feet on their thorax, in addition to some on their abdomen. These feet are called "false" because they don't have joints, but are only sticky stumps.

SKIN
The skin of the caterpillar may be smooth or covered with growths or hair. Its color depends as much on its genes as on what it eats. Many caterpillars mirror the color of the plant on which they are feeding.

CREMASTER
This is the last part of the abdomen of the chrysalis. The cremaster often has hair and hooks that help it hold on to a branch.

ANTENNAE

COMPOUND EYES
The eyes are made up of thousands of small lenses. Each one perceives a part of the image and sends it to the brain. With these eyes, butterflies can see any close movement, no matter how rapid.

RECTUM

DIGESTIVE SYSTEM
The pupa has a smaller intestine than the caterpillar, because it doesn't eat. The anus has no function. It is nothing more than a mark near the cremaster.

STIGMAS
Oxygen is absorbed by the cells of the chrysalis directly from the outside through the stigmas, and not through the blood as in animals with a backbone (like humans).

SPIRAL PROBOSCIS
The mouth of the adult butterfly is like a large straw rolled up into a spiral. In some tropical species, it can measure 6 inches (15cm) in length. It can be unrolled when needed.

HEART

MASTER OF TRANSFORMATION

WING VEINS
The veins in the wings form a network of tubes through which the *hemolymph*, a nerve and respiratory tube, passes. Each group of butterflies has its own distinct pattern of veins.

WINGS
If we were to touch the wings of a butterfly, we would get dust on our hands. This dust that covers the wings is made of crushed hair and it takes the form of scales. The brilliant colors of butterfly wings are due to the pigments of the scales and also to an optical illusion that results from the *diffraction* of light on the scales.

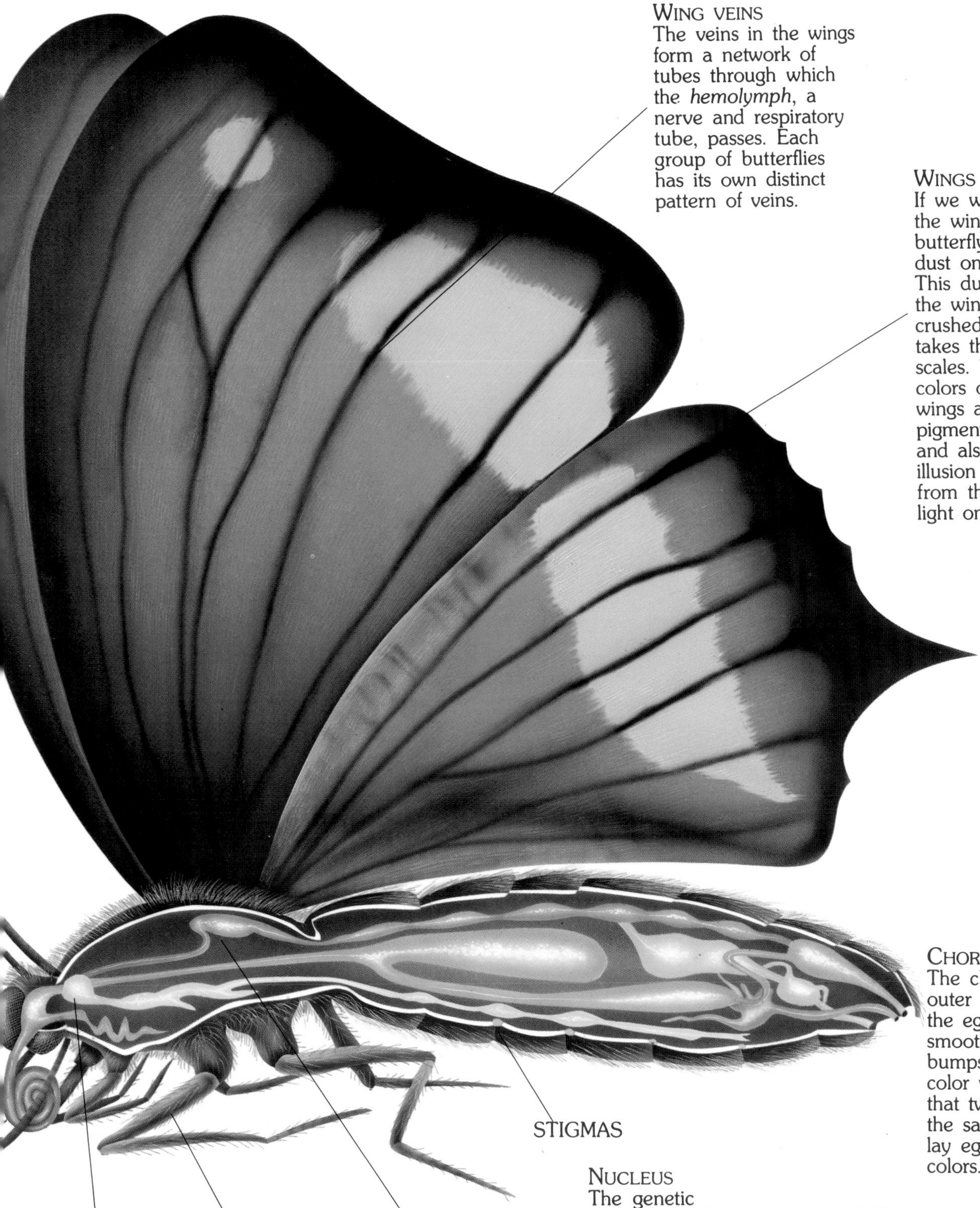

CHORION
The chorion is the outer membrane of the egg. It may be smooth or full of bumps or hair. Its color varies so much that two butterflies of the same species may lay eggs of different colors.

STIGMAS

NUCLEUS
The genetic information that determines everything about the caterpillar, chrysalis and adult stages of each butterfly is found in the nucleus of the egg.

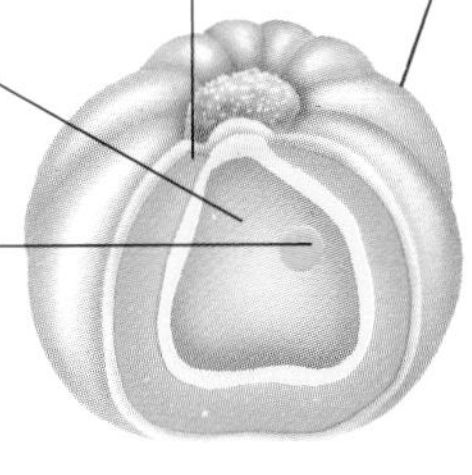

FOOD

STRIPES, RIDGES

BRAIN   LEG   HEART

Ants, like bees and wasps, belong to the order *Hymenoptera*.

Living in a community. Ants are social insects that live in groups or colonies with millions of members.

Worker ants, which are the most numerous, share all the work. There are caregivers that tend the larvae, hunters that search for food and even soldiers that defend the anthill.

One or two queen ants are at the head of the colony. Their only function is to mate with the males and lay eggs. You can tell the males from the workers because they have wings.

Nursery. When mating, the male ants and the queen ant fly in large swarms. Later, the queen lays two different types of eggs: unfertilized eggs that become male ants, and fertilized eggs that become queens and workers.

The weaver ant. The ant gets its name from its nest, which it weaves out of leaves in the shape of a pouch. The silk thread that it uses is produced by larvae, but first adult ants must carry the larvae to the leaves.

An army of ants. Colonies of ants often change anthills. When they make the move, they form an actual army with millions of soldiers. Worker soldiers with their large mandibles march in columns, carrying their queen in the center to protect her.

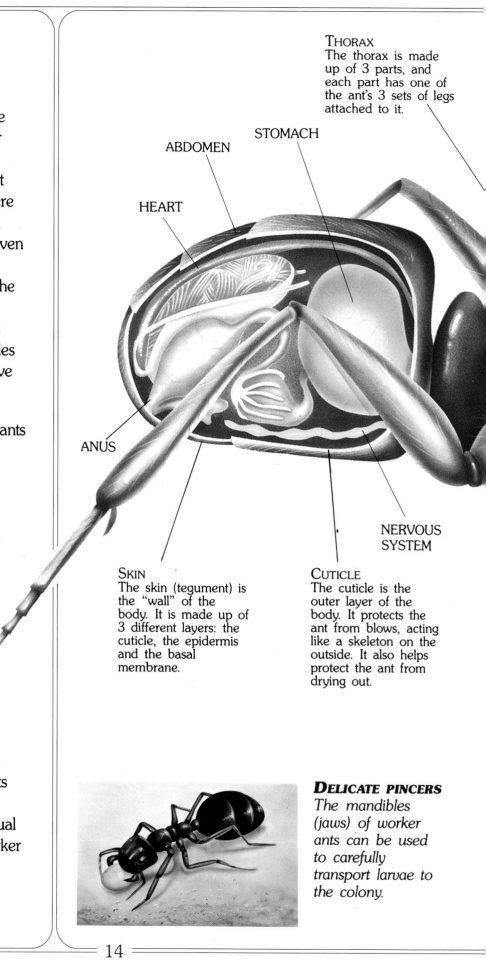

THORAX
The thorax is made up of 3 parts, and each part has one of the ant's 3 sets of legs attached to it.

STOMACH

ABDOMEN

HEART

ANUS

NERVOUS SYSTEM

SKIN
The skin (tegument) is the "wall" of the body. It is made up of 3 different layers: the cuticle, the epidermis and the basal membrane.

CUTICLE
The cuticle is the outer layer of the body. It protects the ant from blows, acting like a skeleton on the outside. It also helps protect the ant from drying out.

DELICATE PINCERS
The mandibles (jaws) of worker ants can be used to carefully transport larvae to the colony.

THE WORKER ANT

HOW THEY BREATHE
Ants breathe through a system of tubes that branch out to circulate air throughout the body.

EYES
The eyes are compound and well developed in many species, but some species have no eyes and the ants are blind.

BRAIN

AORTA

ESOPHAGUS

HEAD
The head has a great range of movement. It can rotate with ease around the ant's narrow neck.

SENSITIVE TIBIA
Many species can detect vibrations through sense organs located on the tibia (lower leg).

MAXILLARY GLANDS

POWERFUL MANDIBLES
The mandibles are strong and capable of chewing, but a lot depends on the species and type of work the ant does. For example, soldier ants have especially large and powerful mandibles.

JOINTED LEGS
The legs are strong, with joints. Each leg has 5 different parts: coxa, tochanter, femur, tibia and tarsus.

OCELLI
In the upper head are 3 simple eyes.

JOHNSTON'S ORGAN
Johnston's Organ is located on the antennae. It helps the ant to keep its balance.

CLAWS
At the end of each foot, there are claws that help the ant move on vertical surfaces.

ANTENNAE
Antennae are in the shape of an elbow. They help to detect chemical and mechanical stimuli.

Fleas are wingless insects that live as *parasites* on birds and mammals. The largest fleas are about ¼ of an inch (8mm) long, but most measure less than half that size. They are usually a dark brown color and their bodies are flattened on the sides, which eases their movements between a host's hair and skin.

Champion jumpers. The rear legs of the flea are very large in comparison to its body. As the flea prepares to jump, it bends its hind legs and then, suddenly, stretches them at the moment of take-off. This action, combined with the lightness of its body, makes for jumps that are very long in relation to the size of the flea.

Permanent housing. Each species of flea has its own host, that is, an animal on which it likes to live. This does not, however, keep it from occasionally attacking another species.

A home like no other. When it is time to reproduce, the flea lays her eggs on the host. From these eggs come small larvae similar to worms.

The small larvae are ravenously hungry. They will eat any food found in the nest, but only if the host is the type of animal on which the flea species can reproduce.

This is how larvae get the type of food and environment they need for their development.

Larvae in the nest then go through a second cycle of metamorphosis and become adult fleas.

ANTENNAE
The organs of smell are located on the flea's antennae. When at rest, the antennae withdraw into a narrow groove.

HEAD
The head is shaped like a triangle. It is narrow in front so that the flea is able to move, like a ship on water, through the hair of the host.

BRAIN

PHARYNX

EYES
The eyes of the flea are not well developed, and its vision is not very good. Some species are blind, especially those that live on hosts that are nocturnal or live underground.

STINGING PROBOSCIS
The mouthparts of the flea slant down and back. They sting the host and suck its blood.

MOUTHPARTS

MALE AND FEMALE FLEAS
You can tell male and female fleas apart by the shape of the head. The antennae of male fleas, for example, are very developed because they have a special role during mating.

MALE FLEA

FEMALE FLEA

THE FLEA: A PARASITE

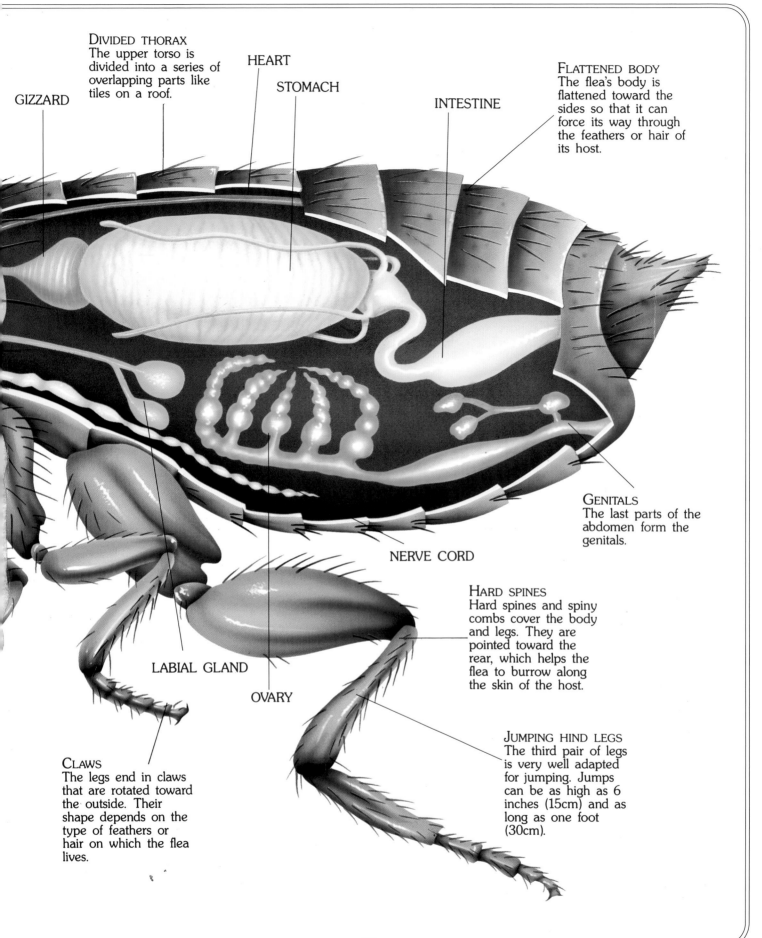

DIVIDED THORAX
The upper torso is divided into a series of overlapping parts like tiles on a roof.

HEART

STOMACH

GIZZARD

INTESTINE

FLATTENED BODY
The flea's body is flattened toward the sides so that it can force its way through the feathers or hair of its host.

GENITALS
The last parts of the abdomen form the genitals.

NERVE CORD

HARD SPINES
Hard spines and spiny combs cover the body and legs. They are pointed toward the rear, which helps the flea to burrow along the skin of the host.

LABIAL GLAND

OVARY

CLAWS
The legs end in claws that are rotated toward the outside. Their shape depends on the type of feathers or hair on which the flea lives.

JUMPING HIND LEGS
The third pair of legs is very well adapted for jumping. Jumps can be as high as 6 inches (15cm) and as long as one foot (30cm).

S piders belong to the order *Arachnida*, which is made up of more than 50,000 different species, including spiders, mites, scorpions, and ticks.

To weave a trap. The spider is one of the few animals in the world that is capable of making its own trap with which to catch insects.

The trap is constructed using a sticky, silky liquid secreted through openings underneath the spider's body.

The silk threads are very thin, 0.003 of a millimeter in diameter, but they are 3 times stronger than a steel thread of equal thickness.

Packing a lunch. When an insect falls into its web, the spider quickly throws itself on top of the insect so that it can't move and wraps it in threads. The spider does this so skillfully that its movements don't destroy the web.

Since spiders are not able to eat solid food, they fill the body of the insect with digestive liquids that break down the victim's tissues. Later, they will leisurely suck out the liquid.

Submarine spiders. Almost all spiders live on dry land, though some can walk on the surface of water. Only one species of spider lives underwater. Its dwellingplace is a network of silk threads filled with air bubbles that hug the surface. Each time the spider leaves the nest to hunt small fish, it carries a small air bubble with it. This bubble performs in the way an air tank does for deep-sea divers.

2, 4, 6, 8 . . . EYES

Spiders that hunt by leaping on their prey have very well developed eyesight. For other species, it is less important; some spiders are blind. Spiders can have 2, 4, 6 or 8 simple eyes.

CHELICERAE
The spider uses the chelicerae to crush its food. Located on both sides of the mouth, these pincer-like appendages end in hollow fangs. Poison is also injected through them.

ESOPHAGUS

POISON DUCT

BRAIN

MOUTH

PEDIPALP
Located on either side of the mouth, these parts are like small legs that grope for, touch and hold food.

SUCKING STOMACH
Since spiders cannot eat anything solid, they crush their food and fill it with digestive juices that break down the tissues. Then the dissolved food is sucked into the stomach.

THE SPIDER: WEAVER OF TRAPS

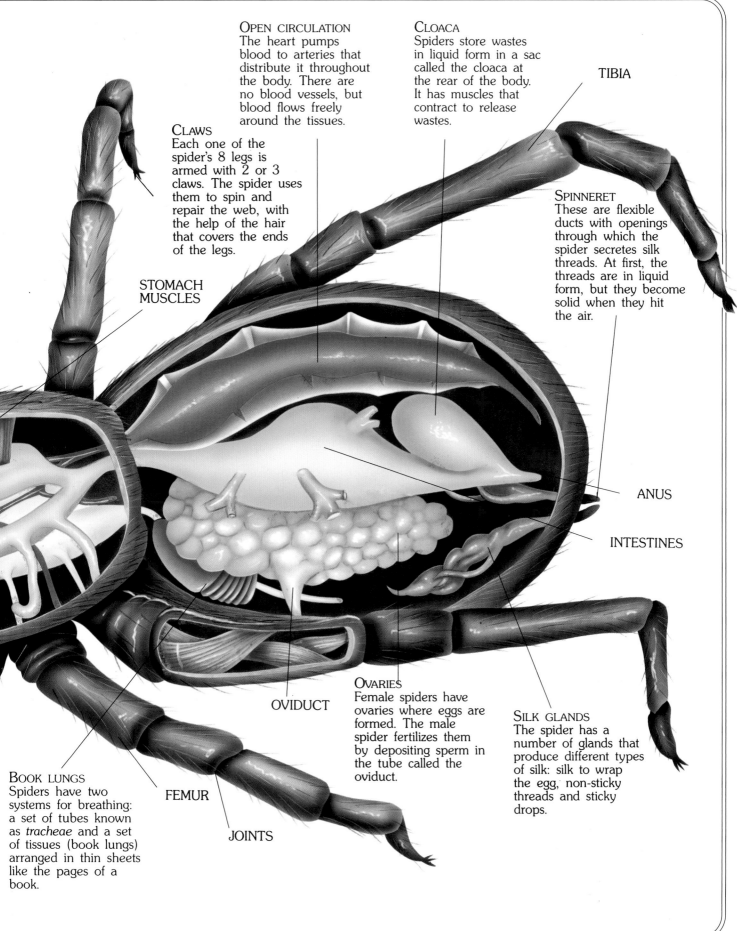

OPEN CIRCULATION
The heart pumps blood to arteries that distribute it throughout the body. There are no blood vessels, but blood flows freely around the tissues.

CLOACA
Spiders store wastes in liquid form in a sac called the cloaca at the rear of the body. It has muscles that contract to release wastes.

TIBIA

CLAWS
Each one of the spider's 8 legs is armed with 2 or 3 claws. The spider uses them to spin and repair the web, with the help of the hair that covers the ends of the legs.

SPINNERET
These are flexible ducts with openings through which the spider secretes silk threads. At first, the threads are in liquid form, but they become solid when they hit the air.

STOMACH MUSCLES

ANUS

INTESTINES

OVARIES
Female spiders have ovaries where eggs are formed. The male spider fertilizes them by depositing sperm in the tube called the oviduct.

OVIDUCT

SILK GLANDS
The spider has a number of glands that produce different types of silk: silk to wrap the egg, non-sticky threads and sticky drops.

FEMUR

BOOK LUNGS
Spiders have two systems for breathing: a set of tubes known as *tracheae* and a set of tissues (book lungs) arranged in thin sheets like the pages of a book.

JOINTS

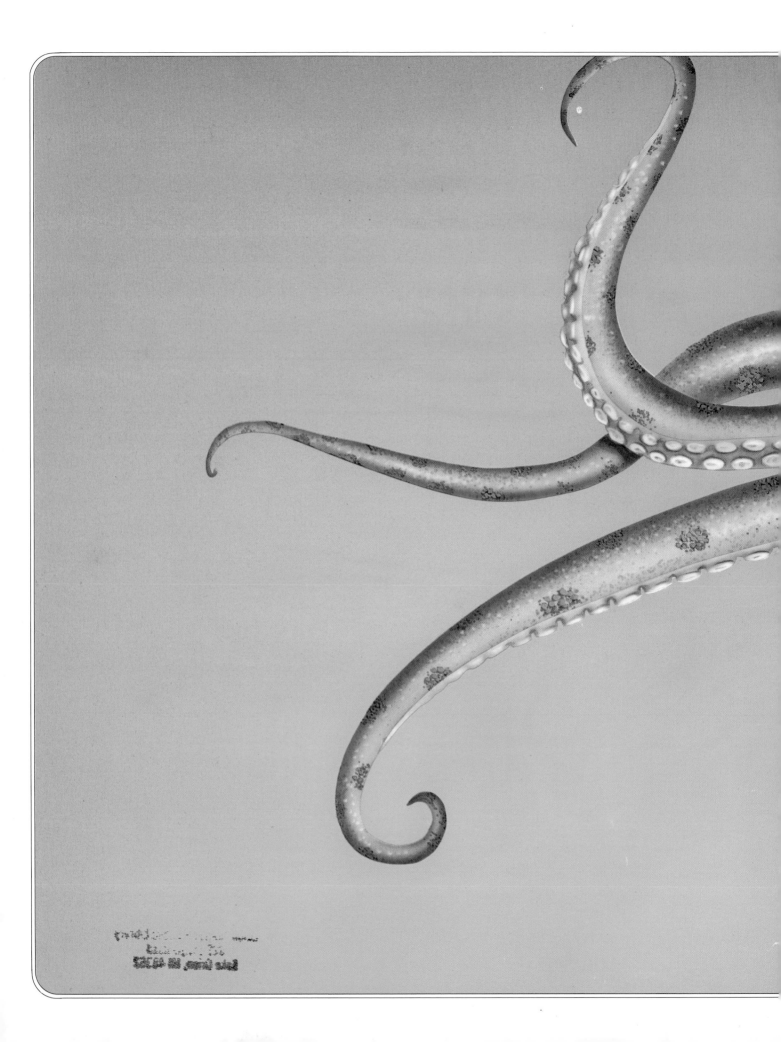

Other invertebrates

All invertebrates lack a spinal column. But many of them do have
some kind of skeleton, shell or protective "shield." More than 90
percent of all animals are invertebrates, including an incredible
array of life forms, from insects to spiders—which you have seen
in the previous chapter—to sponges, jellyfish, centipedes, crabs,
mussels, octopuses and sea urchins.

Octopuses belong to the class *Cephalopoda*, which means "feet on the head" and illustrates one of their main features. All octopuses have arms or tentacles surrounding the head, and they seem to lack a body. What appears, however, to be just an enormous head is in reality the most important part of its strange body. Inside it there are a heart and respiratory and digestive systems.

Octopuses live in all the oceans and in most parts of the sea.

A strange way to swim. The octopus swims as well as most fish. To do this, it has developed a kind of jet propulsion. This system is not only ideal for short spurts at great speed, but also for long distances that demand much endurance.

It works like this: Through openings located on each side of the head, the octopus takes in water that is then shot out through a siphon, a funnel-shaped tube situated on the head.

As the water leaves the siphon, the octopus is suddenly propelled at great speed in the opposite direction. Since the siphon is very flexible, the octopus can move in any direction.

Hidden under a cloud of ink. Another strange feature of the octopus is the sac of ink located near the anus. The ink is a thick black liquid that irritates the eyes and the respiratory organs of other predators.

When the octopus feels threatened, it releases a cloud of black liquid and races away at top speed.

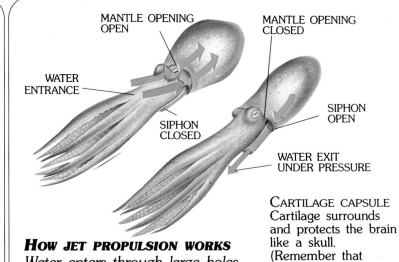

MANTLE OPENING OPEN

MANTLE OPENING CLOSED

WATER ENTRANCE

SIPHON CLOSED

SIPHON OPEN

WATER EXIT UNDER PRESSURE

How jet propulsion works

Water enters through large holes on both sides of the head of the octopus. Meanwhile, the siphon remains closed. When the muscles of the mantle contract, the pressure forces water through the siphon, and the octopus moves rapidly in the opposite direction.

CARTILAGE CAPSULE
Cartilage surrounds and protects the brain like a skull. (Remember that octopuses are invertebrates and have no bones.)

EYES
These are very large with a structure similar to humans'. The octopus can see clearly under water.

PARROT'S BEAK
The mouth of an octopus is shaped like a backwards parrot's beak. Because of powerful muscles surrounding its mouth, the octopus has a strong bite.

SUCKERS
Each sucker has two muscular rings. When the suckers contract against a surface, they stick to it.

PRIMARY LEFT ARM

THE OCTOPUS: JET PROPULSION

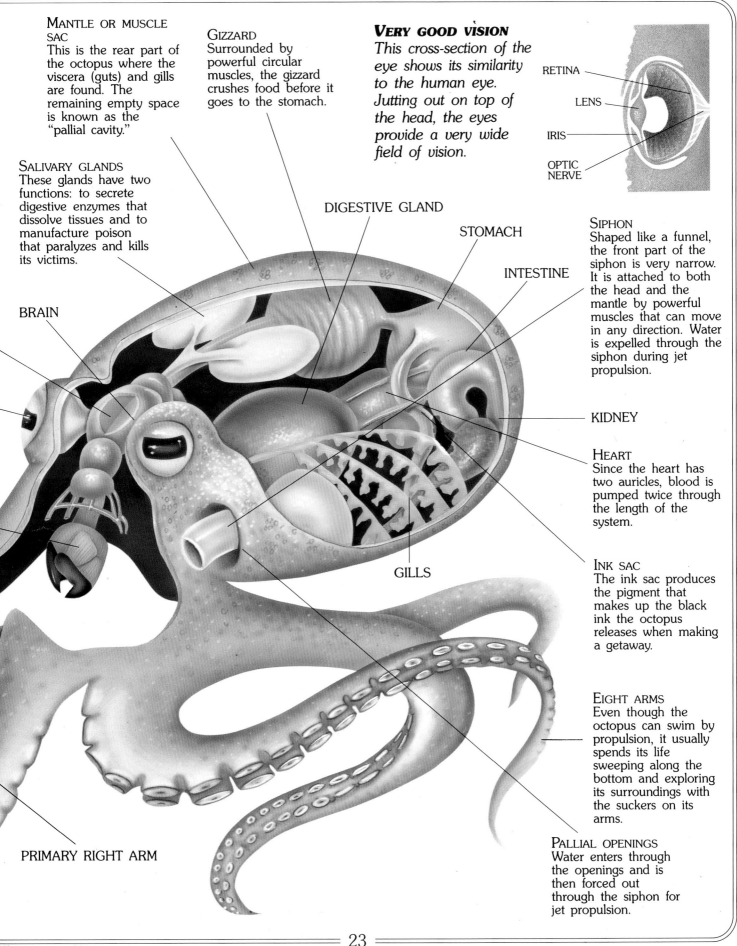

MANTLE OR MUSCLE SAC
This is the rear part of the octopus where the viscera (guts) and gills are found. The remaining empty space is known as the "pallial cavity."

SALIVARY GLANDS
These glands have two functions: to secrete digestive enzymes that dissolve tissues and to manufacture poison that paralyzes and kills its victims.

BRAIN

GIZZARD
Surrounded by powerful circular muscles, the gizzard crushes food before it goes to the stomach.

VERY GOOD VISION
This cross-section of the eye shows its similarity to the human eye. Jutting out on top of the head, the eyes provide a very wide field of vision.

RETINA
LENS
IRIS
OPTIC NERVE

DIGESTIVE GLAND

STOMACH

INTESTINE

SIPHON
Shaped like a funnel, the front part of the siphon is very narrow. It is attached to both the head and the mantle by powerful muscles that can move in any direction. Water is expelled through the siphon during jet propulsion.

KIDNEY

HEART
Since the heart has two auricles, blood is pumped twice through the length of the system.

GILLS

INK SAC
The ink sac produces the pigment that makes up the black ink the octopus releases when making a getaway.

EIGHT ARMS
Even though the octopus can swim by propulsion, it usually spends its life sweeping along the bottom and exploring its surroundings with the suckers on its arms.

PRIMARY RIGHT ARM

PALLIAL OPENINGS
Water enters through the openings and is then forced out through the siphon for jet propulsion.

The giant squid is a *mollusk*. All mollusks have a shell, and here it is internal. This lends stability to the body, which has an aerodynamic shape similar to a torpedo. Like the octopus, a squid has 8 arms, but it also has 2 large tentacles that work together to capture prey.

Living in the depths. Giant squid live at depths of about a mile (1,500m) or more. Absolute darkness and low temperatures prevail on the great plateaus at the bottom of the sea, from about 3¾ miles (6,000m) to the *deeps*, or deepest part of the ocean—about 7 miles (11,000m).

An unknown giant. Almost everything we know about giant squid we have learned through specimens caught in nets. The largest squid ever caught was 66 feet (20m) long and weighed 880 pounds (399kg).

Takes off like an airplane. Like the octopus, the giant squid has a jet propulsion system of movement. This works as water, put under pressure, is expelled through a siphon.
Some small squid fly out of the water, because of the intense thrust of the movement when they launch themselves close to the surface.

Hunter of the deep. Next to the sperm whale, the giant squid is the largest and most powerful hunter in the depths. It moves forward to pursue smaller animals by expelling water under pressure through the siphon, and it reaches out its tentacles just in time to capture its prey.

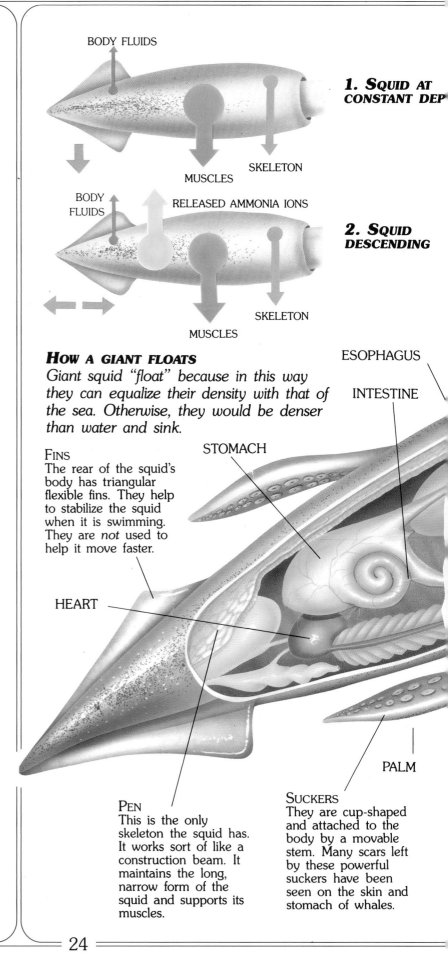

1. SQUID AT CONSTANT DEP[
BODY FLUIDS
MUSCLES
SKELETON

2. SQUID DESCENDING
BODY FLUIDS
RELEASED AMMONIA IONS
MUSCLES
SKELETON

HOW A GIANT FLOATS
Giant squid "float" because in this way they can equalize their density with that of the sea. Otherwise, they would be denser than water and sink.

ESOPHAGUS

INTESTINE

STOMACH

FINS
The rear of the squid's body has triangular flexible fins. They help to stabilize the squid when it is swimming. They are *not* used to help it move faster.

HEART

PEN
This is the only skeleton the squid has. It works sort of like a construction beam. It maintains the long, narrow form of the squid and supports its muscles.

PALM

SUCKERS
They are cup-shaped and attached to the body by a movable stem. Many scars left by these powerful suckers have been seen on the skin and stomach of whales.

THE GIANT SQUID

EYES
Among animals, squid have the largest eyes. They can measure up to 10 inches (25cm) in diameter, larger than a car's headlights. Their eyes are the most advanced among all invertebrates.

HEAD
A giant squid's head is enormous—about 3.3 feet (1m) in length. It contains the mouth of the squid surrounded by eight thick arms and two large, thin tentacles.

RADULA
Like a nail file, the radula is a scraper-like tongue with rows of sharp teeth. The beak-like mandible breaks food into pieces while the radula pushes it toward the stomach.

PARROT'S BEAK
The mandibles of the squid look like a parrot's beak. The upper mandible is sharp-edged and, along with the lower, forms a cutting surface like a razor.

INK SAC
When squid sense danger, they release a cloud of black liquid through the anus to confuse their enemies. The ink of some squid that live in dark waters is luminous, so that it blinds predators, allowing the squid to escape.

ARMS
The squid has 8 arms plus 2 tentacles. Its arms are much shorter than its tentacles. Each arm has 2 rows of suckers that become smaller toward the end. Male squid have 2 arms that are used in reproduction, but they are different from their regular arms.

BRAIN

ANUS

DIGESTIVE GLAND

TENTACLES
Two large tentacles work like pincers when squid capture prey. Each one has a wider area—the palm—that has suckers on it and small sticky projections.

SIPHON
This is the tube used in jet propulsion. As water is shot through it, the squid moves in the opposite direction. The squid can move forward and backward, up and down and toward the sides.

MANTLE
The color of the squid's mantle, or body, ranges from dark red to brown on its back. It is whiter underneath. It can change color depending upon water conditions or the amount of light.

GILLS
Squid breathe through a pair of large gills that look like combs. Water surrounding the gills constantly flows in and out of the pallial cavity, with the movement of the squid's muscles.

SUCKERS LIKE CLAWS
Giant squid have suckers that are capable of immobilizing their prey and can even leave scars on the skin of whales.

Mussels are *mollusks* in the order of *bivalves* that includes cockles, oysters, razor clams and other inhabitants of fresh and salt water. What they all have in common is a hard protective two-piece shell.

An impregnable fortress. The shell of a mussel is made of two halves, or valves, joined on each end by a type of hinge. For the mussel, this shell is a very safe dwelling, because it can seal itself off from all predators. The mussel can filter out particles of food from water and absorb the water at the same time. It gets rid of wastes through ducts called siphons.

A house that walks. In spite of the fact that it is attached to a hard shell, the mussel can move along the bottom of the ocean. It manages this by using an organ called the "foot," a long muscle on which it travels.

Sticking to the rocks. The muscle that makes up the foot has long, strong cords that firmly attach the mussel to the rocks in places where it lives. Larval mussels attach themselves to rocks shortly after they hatch out of the egg.

LEAVING THE SHELL
If you looked at a mussel without its shell, you would see a soft body with no skeleton or spine.

HINGE
This hinge works the way gears do. The teeth of one part of the shell mesh with those of the other. In mussels, there is very little movement possible at the hinge. The valves connect mostly by ligaments that bind them together.

HEPATOPANCREAS

HEART

KIDNEY

FOOT
The organ by which the mussel moves has the shape of a hatchet. The shape of the foot helps the mussel to anchor itself to rocks, wood, and so on, in areas of strong waves.

LIP PALPI
These are located around the edge of the mantle. They create water currents that will drag food toward the mouth of the mussel.

THE ARMOR-CLAD MUSSEL

MANTLE
The mantle covers the back of the bivalve's body. It produces the shell. It is made of 2 parts—each part produces half of the outer shell.

GILLS
Respiration is accomplished through 2 gills that lie between the mantle and the body of the mussel.

SENSE ORGANS
The sensory organs are limited and are composed of only sensory cells shared by the entire mantle and especially abundant along its edge.

LIGAMENT
The ligament is a kind of cord that helps to hold the two parts of the shell together. It is very elastic, which allows the shell to close.

ADDUCTOR MUSCLES
The adductor muscles work to pull the shells shut. When they are relaxed, the valves stay open.

MOUTH

PALLIAL CAVITY

SHELL
The two parts of the shell are usually symmetrical.

BYSSUS
This is a liquid that runs down a groove in the foot. When it solidifies, it will form a thread that attaches the mussel to a rock.

LIKE STALACTITES IN A CAVERN
Some shells look extraordinarily beautiful inside, like the spectacular forms that hang down from the top of a cave.

Lobsters are *crustaceans*, a group that also includes crayfish, crabs, shrimp, and a vast number of small animals, such as the water flea.

Well armed. Lobsters have 5 pairs of legs. The front pair end in thick pincers. The lobster uses them to trap prey and then place it in the mouth, where it can be crushed by the jaws.

A strange way to walk. When crustaceans move around on land, they walk sideways. They may even walk backwards if fleeing from danger.

Many species that live in water sometimes use the rear pair of legs like oars when swimming.

An unwelcome guest. Almost all species of crustacean are protected by a hard shell. The species that don't have a shell find a way to get one. It's sort of like moving into someone else's house.

The hermit crab, for example, has a habit of walking into empty snail shells looking for protection. If the shell is not empty, the crab will not hesitate to kill the snail and take over its shell. As a result, the hermit crab not only gets a home, but finds food as well.

A climbing crab. The robber crab is a land crab with the peculiar habit of climbing palm trees. It works its way up the tree trunk, holding on with its pincers, and eats the meat of the coconuts. Once it has a full stomach, it has no desire to return to the ground by the same route. The crab just lets itself fall from the tree.

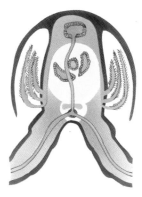

RESPIRATORY SYSTEM
As you can see, the gills, which the lobster uses to get oxygen, are set inside gill chambers that are underneath the shell toward the front part of the body.

HEART
The circulatory system is formed by a tube located above the digestive tube. It occupies an area larger than the heart.

GREEN GLANDS
Most lobster excretions are carried out by a pair of green glands found at the base of the antennae.

EYES
Lobsters can see through 2 compound eyes that can move around with great ease. Each one is made up of hundreds of simple eyes.

ANTENNAE
These whip-like filaments can be very long. They are covered with short "hairs" that enable the lobster to detect chemicals, food and other changes in the environment.

ROSTRUM

ANTENNULES
Follow these 2 joined filaments to their bases. There you'll find 2 organs of equilibrium with a small opening to the outside. Hearing and balance depend on these organs.

ESOPHAGUS

MOUTHPARTS
Six pairs of mouth-parts, located on both sides of the mouth, are used for chewing. They include the mandibles, maxillae and maxillipeds.

THE LOBSTER & ITS RELATIVES

HEPATOPANCREAS
This is a digestive gland that doubles as liver and pancreas. It is located on both sides of the stomach.

ABDOMEN
The abdomen is very flexible, since it is formed by 6 interconnected rings. This allows the abdomen to fold under the cephalothorax.

SHELL
The outer body is protected by a hard shell that is a very tough piece of armor. It covers the 3 parts of the lobster's body: the cephalothorax, abdomen and telson.

CEPHALOTHORAX
The front part of the body is called the cephalothorax. Quite long, it ends in a sharp point. It contains the legs.

INTESTINE

TELSON
The telson is made up of 2 parts that form the tail fin. When attacked, the lobster may move backwards while rapidly beating its tail fin under its abdomen.

MOVEMENT
The river crayfish moves slowly, using its 4 pairs of rear legs. The front pair is used only to obtain food.

TESTICLE

MOUTH

GILLS
The lobster gets air through gills located under the shell. To help this along, the lobster moves some of its limbs to create a water current toward the gills.

A VERY PROTECTIVE MOTHER
Fertilized eggs are attached to the underside of the lobster's abdomen. This protects them from predators.

ponges are the most primitive multicellular organisms. Most of the 3,000 species live in the sea, while only about 150 are freshwater species.

An animal that looks like a plant. Unlike most animals, sponges cannot move. They are permanently attached to the ocean floor or rocks. They look a lot like plants. Actually, for many years it was believed that they *were* plants. It wasn't until 1765 that scientists discovered that sponges were animals.

Filters of the sea. The body of the sponge is formed by many cells clustered around a skeleton.

The cell walls are filled with countless pores. Water from the sea and rivers where the sponges live enters through these pores and flows into a large interior chamber. It is expelled through a wide opening after food and oxygen have been extracted from it.

Blind and deaf. The entire body of a sponge is a filter that takes nutrients out of the water.

It has no eyes or ears or any other senses. There is no nervous system.

Bath sponges. Most bath sponges today are artificial, manufactured with the same material used for man-made silk production. But, for many years, bath sponges were natural ones taken from the skeletons of certain species.

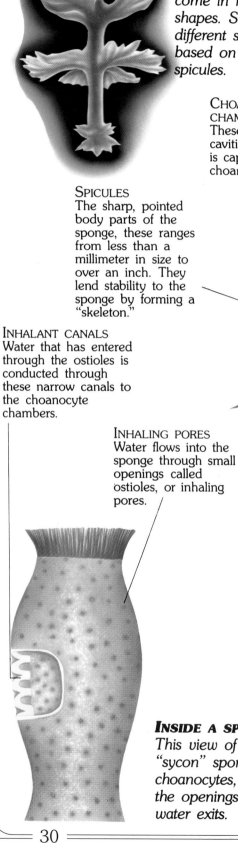

MANY TYPES OF SPONGE
The sponge's sharp, pointed body parts, called spicules, come in many different shapes. Scientists classify different species of sponges based on the shape of their spicules.

CHOANOCYTE CHAMBERS
These are large cavities in which food is captured by the choanocytes.

SPICULES
The sharp, pointed body parts of the sponge, these ranges from less than a millimeter in size to over an inch. They lend stability to the sponge by forming a "skeleton."

INHALANT CANALS
Water that has entered through the ostioles is conducted through these narrow canals to the choanocyte chambers.

INHALING PORES
Water flows into the sponge through small openings called ostioles, or inhaling pores.

INSIDE A SPONGE
This view of the inside of a "sycon" sponge shows the choanocytes, inhaling canals and the openings through which water exits.

THE SPONGE: A LIVING FILTER

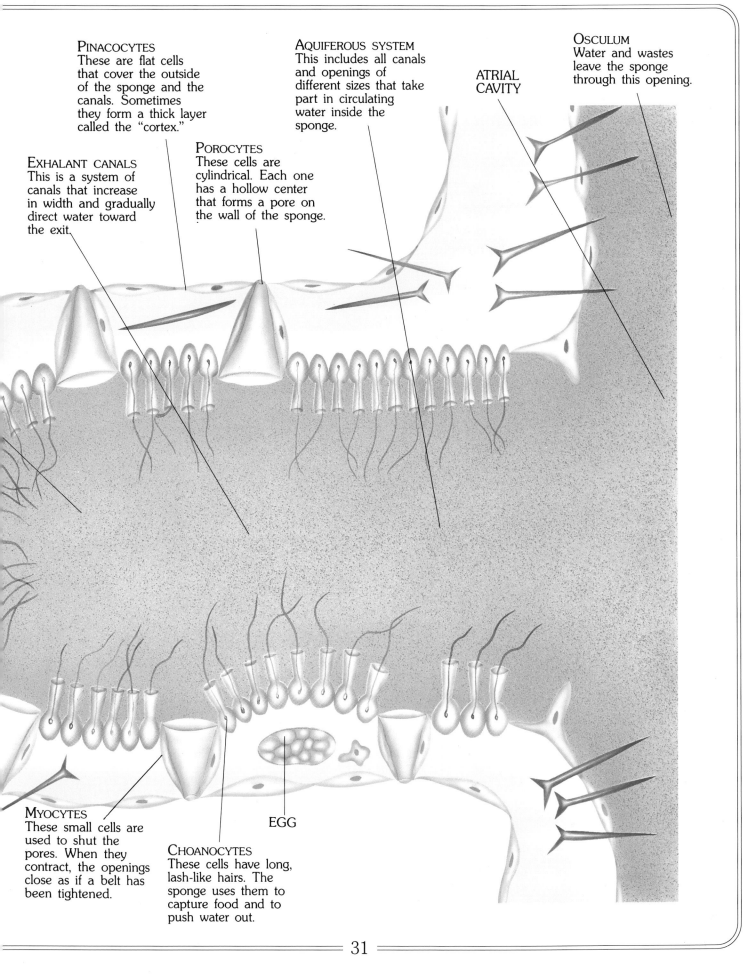

PINACOCYTES
These are flat cells
that cover the outside
of the sponge and the
canals. Sometimes
they form a thick layer
called the "cortex."

AQUIFEROUS SYSTEM
This includes all canals
and openings of
different sizes that take
part in circulating
water inside the
sponge.

OSCULUM
Water and wastes
leave the sponge
through this opening.

ATRIAL
CAVITY

EXHALANT CANALS
This is a system of
canals that increase
in width and gradually
direct water toward
the exit.

POROCYTES
These cells are
cylindrical. Each one
has a hollow center
that forms a pore on
the wall of the sponge.

MYOCYTES
These small cells are
used to shut the
pores. When they
contract, the openings
close as if a belt has
been tightened.

EGG

CHOANOCYTES
These cells have long,
lash-like hairs. The
sponge uses them to
capture food and to
push water out.

THE JELLYFISH:

Jellyfish are *coelenterates*, which, unlike other members of this group—such as coral or sea anemones—do not remain attached to rocks and the bottom of the sea but move around by floating in water.

Almost everything is water. The body of a jellyfish is 99 percent water. Despite having such a soft consistency, it can reach 6½ feet (2m) in diameter.

The most common shape of a jellyfish is that of an umbrella with 4 to 8 tentacles around the edges.

The underside of the body has a short tube that acts as a mouth.

Double reproduction. Jellyfish reproduce in a very peculiar way. Female jellyfish release their *ovules* (eggs) into the sea, where they are fertilized by *spermatozoids* released by male jellyfish.

From the fertilized ovules will emerge larvae that later will settle on a rock and give rise to a colony of *polyps*, another animal form. From these polyps, which are anchored to the bottom by a species of roots, new jellyfish will break away and float into the sea.

A poison dart. Jellyfish have a great number of cells that produce substances that itch and have a stinger inside. Should an animal accidentally touch one of the tentacles of the jellyfish, these cells fire off, like poisonous darts. After they enter the body of the victim, the stinger bursts and the poison spreads.

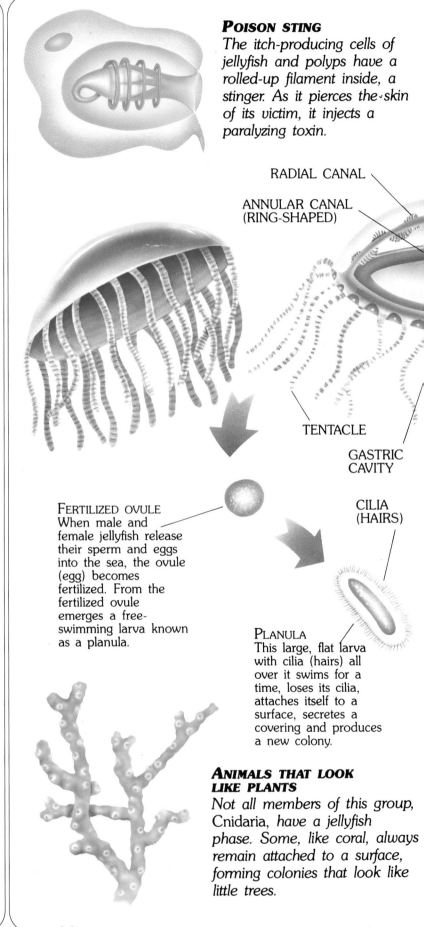

POISON STING
The itch-producing cells of jellyfish and polyps have a rolled-up filament inside, a stinger. As it pierces the skin of its victim, it injects a paralyzing toxin.

RADIAL CANAL

ANNULAR CANAL
(RING-SHAPED)

TENTACLE

GASTRIC CAVITY

CILIA
(HAIRS)

FERTILIZED OVULE
When male and female jellyfish release their sperm and eggs into the sea, the ovule (egg) becomes fertilized. From the fertilized ovule emerges a free-swimming larva known as a planula.

PLANULA
This large, flat larva with cilia (hairs) all over it swims for a time, loses its cilia, attaches itself to a surface, secretes a covering and produces a new colony.

ANIMALS THAT LOOK LIKE PLANTS
Not all members of this group, Cnidaria, have a jellyfish phase. Some, like coral, always remain attached to a surface, forming colonies that look like little trees.

HOW IT REPRODUCES

GONADS
Jellyfish have gonads and they are the only ones of its biological group to reproduce sexually. Gonads of male jellyfish produce spermatozoids and those of females produce ovules.

NERVOUS SYSTEM
The nervous system of the jellyfish is formed by two rings, one inside and one outside. These rings stimulate the tentacles, senses and muscles.

STATOCYSTS
Among the tentacles, are statocysts, which are formed by a mineral deposit with cilia, small hairs that move when touched. Depending on which cilia is touched, the animal contracts to straighten itself.

MOUTH

TENTACLE
Polyps and jellyfish have fringe-like tentacles with itch-producing cells surrounding the mouth. These are used to paralyze their victims and then place them in the mouth.

HYDROTHECA
The entire colony is covered by an outer skeleton called the hydrotheca. Those who defend and feed the colony can pull out their tentacles through an opening.

REPRODUCTIVE POLYP

MANUBRIUM

OCELLI (EYES)
Ocelli are the sight organs of jellyfish, found at the base of the tentacles. They cannot distinguish shapes but only light intensity.

JELLYFISH BUD

FEEDING POLYP
In a polyps colony, work is shared. Those in charge of capturing and digesting prey for the entire colony are called feeding polyps.

FREE-FLOATING JELLYFISH
Jellyfish are shaped like umbrellas. In what would be the handle, a wide cylinder hangs called the manubrium. At the end of it a mouth opens to the outside.

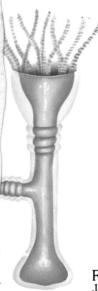

REPRODUCTIVE POLYP
Jellyfish begin as buds on reproductive polyps, much like the shoots on a plant. The jellyfish break away into the water.

STOLON
Each member of the colony is connected to the others, and all are anchored to a surface by a stolon, a type of root spread over marine rocks.

GASTROVASCULAR CAVITY
The stomach of a polyp is a sac with an opening for food to enter and wastes to leave. Food is digested there and then distributed to all the members of the colony.

CARNIVORE OF THE SEA

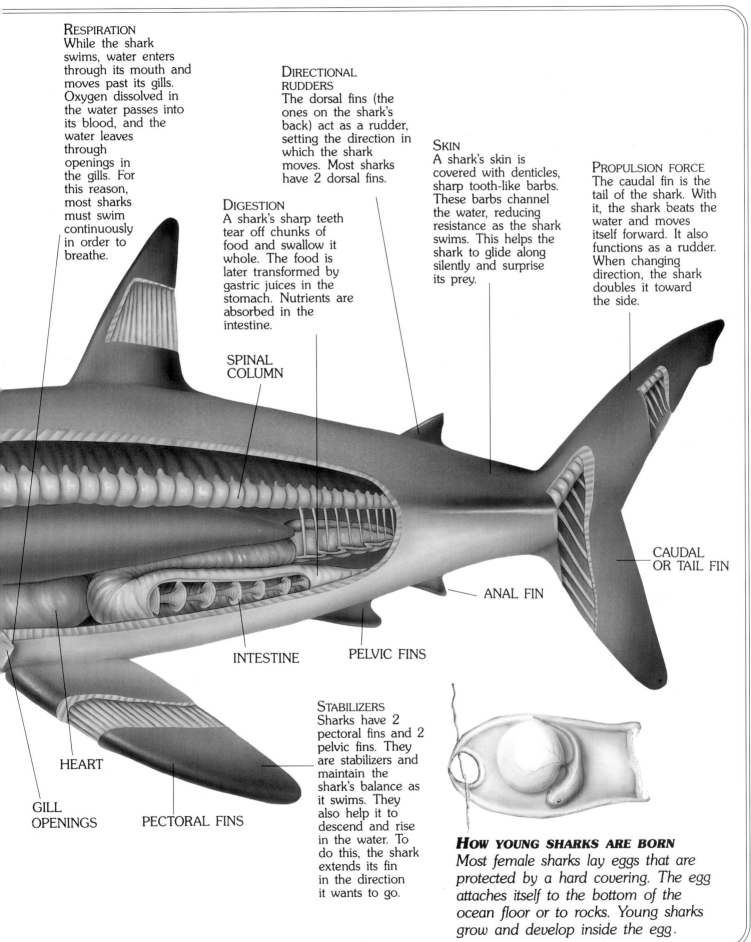

RESPIRATION
While the shark swims, water enters through its mouth and moves past its gills. Oxygen dissolved in the water passes into its blood, and the water leaves through openings in the gills. For this reason, most sharks must swim continuously in order to breathe.

DIRECTIONAL RUDDERS
The dorsal fins (the ones on the shark's back) act as a rudder, setting the direction in which the shark moves. Most sharks have 2 dorsal fins.

DIGESTION
A shark's sharp teeth tear off chunks of food and swallow it whole. The food is later transformed by gastric juices in the stomach. Nutrients are absorbed in the intestine.

SKIN
A shark's skin is covered with denticles, sharp tooth-like barbs. These barbs channel the water, reducing resistance as the shark swims. This helps the shark to glide along silently and surprise its prey.

PROPULSION FORCE
The caudal fin is the tail of the shark. With it, the shark beats the water and moves itself forward. It also functions as a rudder. When changing direction, the shark doubles it toward the side.

SPINAL COLUMN

CAUDAL OR TAIL FIN

ANAL FIN

INTESTINE

PELVIC FINS

STABILIZERS
Sharks have 2 pectoral fins and 2 pelvic fins. They are stabilizers and maintain the shark's balance as it swims. They also help it to descend and rise in the water. To do this, the shark extends its fin in the direction it wants to go.

HEART

GILL OPENINGS

PECTORAL FINS

HOW YOUNG SHARKS ARE BORN
Most female sharks lay eggs that are protected by a hard covering. The egg attaches itself to the bottom of the ocean floor or to rocks. Young sharks grow and develop inside the egg.

ony fish make up the largest group in the fish family. Most common fish that populate the seas and rivers are bony fish, such as tuna, sardines, swordfish, salmon, and so on. They all have skeletons made of bone.

Champion swimmers. Most bony fish have a sleek, spindle-shaped body, a form that is especially good for fast swimming. Their fins also help them to maneuver easily in water, which makes most of them champion swimmers.

The fins can be propellers to move them forward, stabilizers to prevent their rolling from side to side and rudders to assist in changes of direction.

The fastest fish in the sea. Because of their spindle-shaped body and sleek tail fin in the shape of a half-moon, some of the best swimmers in the sea are the swordfish and sailfish. The swordfish is one of the fastest. When pursuing prey, it may swim at speeds of 50 miles (80km) per hour and it is capable of reaching 80 miles (130km) per hour to make a surprise attack on an unsuspecting catch.

The largest fish. The largest fish is the whale shark, which can get as long as 56 feet (17m) and weigh 38½ tons (35,000kg).

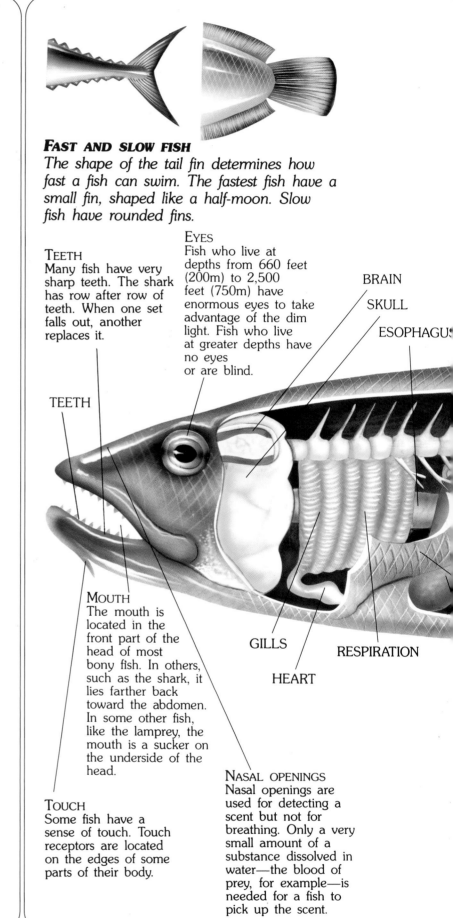

FAST AND SLOW FISH
The shape of the tail fin determines how fast a fish can swim. The fastest fish have a small fin, shaped like a half-moon. Slow fish have rounded fins.

TEETH
Many fish have very sharp teeth. The shark has row after row of teeth. When one set falls out, another replaces it.

EYES
Fish who live at depths from 660 feet (200m) to 2,500 feet (750m) have enormous eyes to take advantage of the dim light. Fish who live at greater depths have no eyes or are blind.

BRAIN

SKULL

ESOPHAGUS

TEETH

MOUTH
The mouth is located in the front part of the head of most bony fish. In others, such as the shark, it lies farther back toward the abdomen. In some other fish, like the lamprey, the mouth is a sucker on the underside of the head.

GILLS

RESPIRATION

HEART

TOUCH
Some fish have a sense of touch. Touch receptors are located on the edges of some parts of their body.

NASAL OPENINGS
Nasal openings are used for detecting a scent but not for breathing. Only a very small amount of a substance dissolved in water—the blood of prey, for example—is needed for a fish to pick up the scent.

THE TUNA: A BONY FISH

WHAT THEY EAT
Fish eat plankton, which is made up of tiny plants and animals. Some of them also eat other fish, mollusks, such as mussels, and crustaceans, such as shrimps. The fish who eat mollusks and crustaceans live at the bottom of the sea. The fish who eat plankton are eaten by larger fish.

LATERAL LINE
Most fish have the organ called the lateral line. It is filled with nerve endings through which the fish can sense vibrations in the water. When waves bounce off an object—such as a rock or prey—the lateral line is able to detect its size and location.

OPERCULUM

SPINAL COLUMN

EGGS
Almost all female fish lay eggs. Some just lay them in the water, where millions of eggs may float until little fish hatch. Some fish, such as some female sharks, don't lay eggs at all, but give birth to young that are already formed.

KIDNEY

SWIM BLADDER

INTESTINE

STOMACH

DIGESTION
Food is eased toward the fish's stomach by its esophagus, which is very elastic. Some fish eat large prey and have stomachs that crush food. Later the food travels on into the intestine.

OPERCULUM
A bony plate called the operculum protects the gills of bony fish. Other fish, such as sharks and rays, have several openings in the flesh over the gills without an operculum to protect them.

LIVER

LIKE RIBS OF A FAN
Fins stick out from the body of a fish in the shape of a fan. They are supported by ribs called "radials." There are many radials and they are joined side by side.

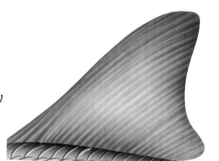

Rays are fish with a short, flattened body and a long tail. Like sharks and sawfish, they are classified as cartilaginous fish because they have a skeleton of cartilage. Rays live at the bottom of marine waters. This is why their bodies have a flat shape. They also have very developed pectoral fins that can easily span 6½ feet (2m). Because of these large fins, they seem to fly through the water.

Hunting by electric charge. The capability of some animals to give off electrical charges is not only an efficient defense mechanism, but it is also a way to capture prey without much movement. The electric ray, for example, stays hidden and buried in the sand. At the right moment it "connects the batteries" and stuns or kills its prey. Afterwards, in safety, the fish covers its catch with its wide, flat body and devours it.

Birth in a capsule. Female rays are oviparous (egg-layers). They lay their eggs during the summer, and the young are born fully developed in semi-transparent capsules. These capsules remain attached to algae and rocks by strong filaments located on the corners.

Poisonous tails. The ray's major food source is crustaceans, whose shells are easily broken by the ray's strong teeth. Many rays have whip-like tails with which they strike their prey. Some of these tails have poison stingers on the ends.

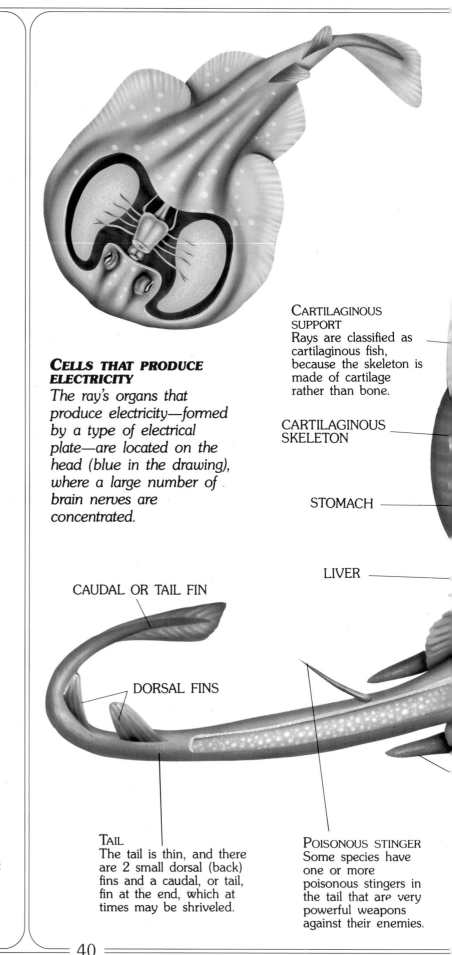

CELLS THAT PRODUCE ELECTRICITY
The ray's organs that produce electricity—formed by a type of electrical plate—are located on the head (blue in the drawing), where a large number of brain nerves are concentrated.

CARTILAGINOUS SUPPORT
Rays are classified as cartilaginous fish, because the skeleton is made of cartilage rather than bone.

CARTILAGINOUS SKELETON

STOMACH

LIVER

CAUDAL OR TAIL FIN

DORSAL FINS

TAIL
The tail is thin, and there are 2 small dorsal (back) fins and a caudal, or tail, fin at the end, which at times may be shriveled.

POISONOUS STINGER
Some species have one or more poisonous stingers in the tail that are very powerful weapons against their enemies.

THE RAY: AN ELECTRIC FISH

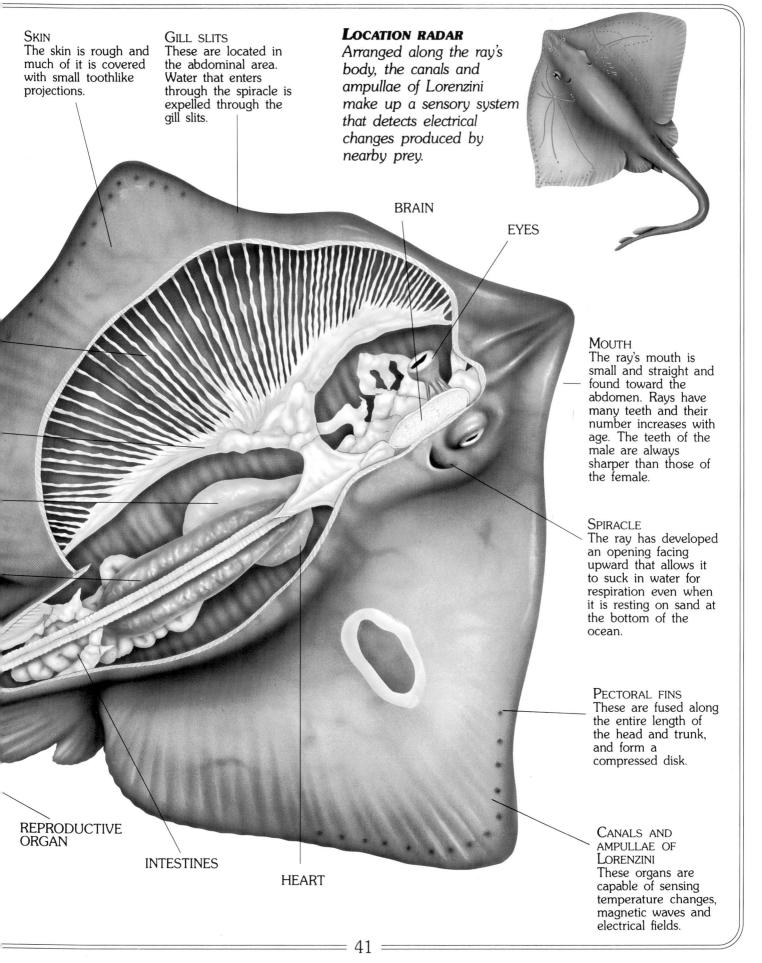

SKIN
The skin is rough and much of it is covered with small toothlike projections.

GILL SLITS
These are located in the abdominal area. Water that enters through the spiracle is expelled through the gill slits.

LOCATION RADAR
Arranged along the ray's body, the canals and ampullae of Lorenzini make up a sensory system that detects electrical changes produced by nearby prey.

BRAIN

EYES

MOUTH
The ray's mouth is small and straight and found toward the abdomen. Rays have many teeth and their number increases with age. The teeth of the male are always sharper than those of the female.

SPIRACLE
The ray has developed an opening facing upward that allows it to suck in water for respiration even when it is resting on sand at the bottom of the ocean.

PECTORAL FINS
These are fused along the entire length of the head and trunk, and form a compressed disk.

REPRODUCTIVE ORGAN

INTESTINES

HEART

CANALS AND AMPULLAE OF LORENZINI
These organs are capable of sensing temperature changes, magnetic waves and electrical fields.

THE SALMON:

The salmon is a bony fish that can measure up to 5 feet (1.5m) long. It lives only in the Atlantic and Pacific Oceans but returns to the rivers to reproduce.

A fish that changes color. A salmon's body is spindle-shaped, like most bony fish. It has thick skin covered with scales and is dark-colored on the back and white on the abdomen. However, as the time to spawn draws near, and the salmon prepare to return to the river, the color of the male salmon changes from dark to a luminous red.

Swimming upstream. At spawning time, male and female salmon begin their long, arduous journey upstream, swimming against the current and overcoming differences in water levels through spectacular jumps. When, at last, they reach the cold, clean waters near the source of the river, the male salmon fertilize the females, and the females deposit their eggs. The adult salmon then return to the sea.

Alone at home. From these eggs emerge tiny larvae that have to fend for themselves. Within 2 years they become fully developed fish about 6 inches (15cm) long. Now they are strong enough to make the same journey as their parents, and they go downstream in search of the sea.

In the ocean, they finish developing and become adults. Like their parents, they will return to the river where they were born to spawn.

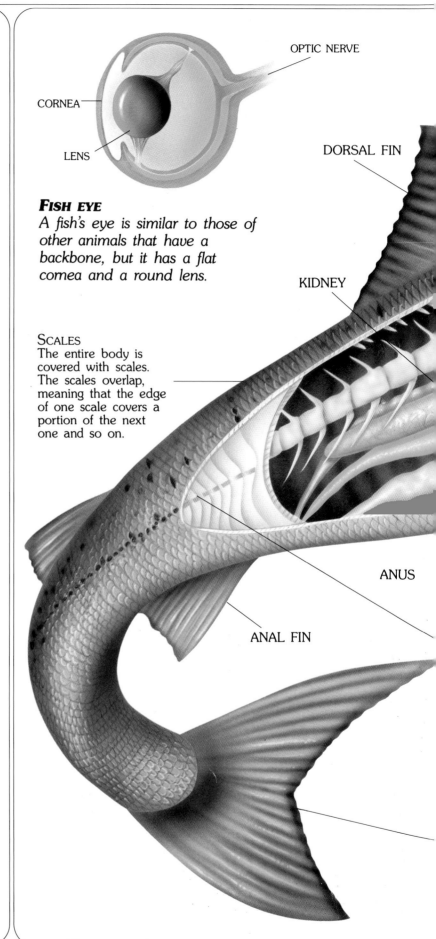

OPTIC NERVE

CORNEA

LENS

FISH EYE
A fish's eye is similar to those of other animals that have a backbone, but it has a flat cornea and a round lens.

DORSAL FIN

KIDNEY

SCALES
The entire body is covered with scales. The scales overlap, meaning that the edge of one scale covers a portion of the next one and so on.

ANUS

ANAL FIN

BETWEEN RIVER AND SEA

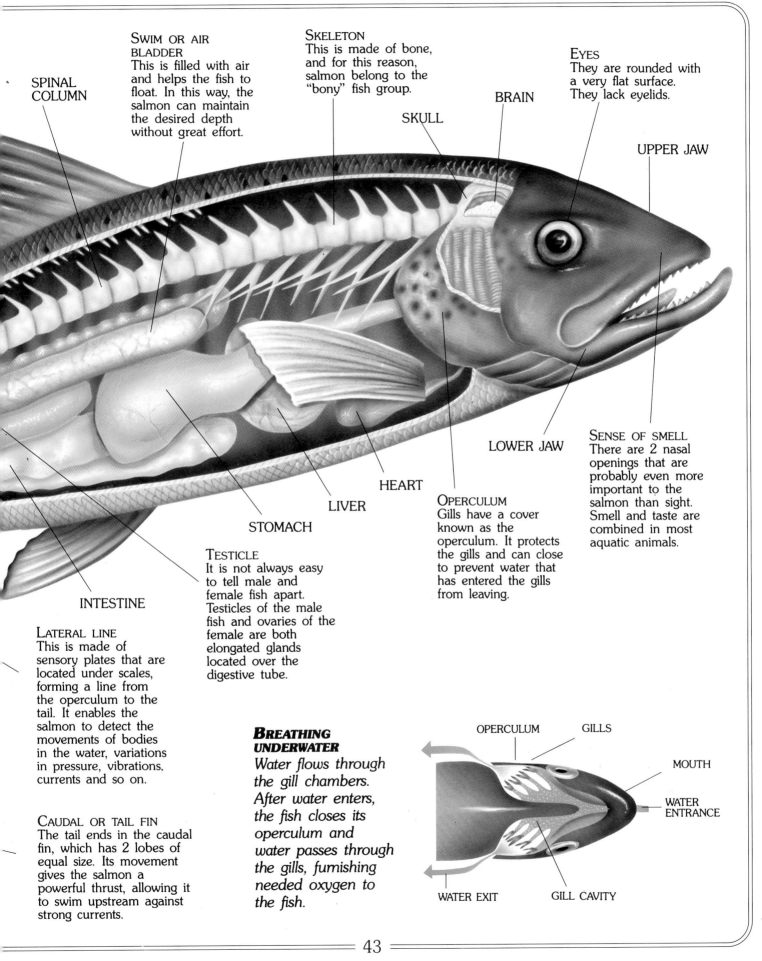

SPINAL COLUMN

SWIM OR AIR BLADDER
This is filled with air and helps the fish to float. In this way, the salmon can maintain the desired depth without great effort.

SKELETON
This is made of bone, and for this reason, salmon belong to the "bony" fish group.

SKULL

BRAIN

EYES
They are rounded with a very flat surface. They lack eyelids.

UPPER JAW

LOWER JAW

SENSE OF SMELL
There are 2 nasal openings that are probably even more important to the salmon than sight. Smell and taste are combined in most aquatic animals.

OPERCULUM
Gills have a cover known as the operculum. It protects the gills and can close to prevent water that has entered the gills from leaving.

HEART

LIVER

STOMACH

TESTICLE
It is not always easy to tell male and female fish apart. Testicles of the male fish and ovaries of the female are both elongated glands located over the digestive tube.

INTESTINE

LATERAL LINE
This is made of sensory plates that are located under scales, forming a line from the operculum to the tail. It enables the salmon to detect the movements of bodies in the water, variations in pressure, vibrations, currents and so on.

CAUDAL OR TAIL FIN
The tail ends in the caudal fin, which has 2 lobes of equal size. Its movement gives the salmon a powerful thrust, allowing it to swim upstream against strong currents.

BREATHING UNDERWATER
Water flows through the gill chambers. After water enters, the fish closes its operculum and water passes through the gills, furnishing needed oxygen to the fish.

OPERCULUM

GILLS

MOUTH

WATER ENTRANCE

WATER EXIT

GILL CAVITY

Amphibians and reptiles

Amphibians live in the water during the tadpole stage of their lives. Once transformed into adults, they spend part of their lives on land, but return to the water, where the females lay their eggs. Reptiles, which evolved from amphibians 300 million years ago, are completely adapted to life on land. They belong to various groups that include turtles, tuatara, lizards, snakes and crocodiles.

Frogs are amphibians, a word that means "double life" and reveals the principal feature of this group of animals, their ability to live in two worlds: land and water.

When frogs croak. When most frogs are ready to reproduce, they form a large group. Male frogs begin to sing, inflating their mouth sacs to get the attention of the females. When a female draws near, the male will quickly mount her back and they mate. Most frogs lay their eggs in water in springtime. There may be anywhere from one to 20,000 eggs, depending on the species. From 5 days to a few weeks later, the eggs hatch.

Metamorphosis. The larva that emerges from each egg has an unformed mouth but gills, like a fish, on both sides of its head. These allow it to breathe underwater. After a few days, the tail grows, the external gills disappear and other gills develop inside the body. It is a tadpole.

Most tadpoles grow from larva to frog in a few months. Front and back legs develop and grow; the mouth position changes; the tadpole breathes through lungs and the tail begins to disappear. The transformation—from larva to tadpole, which lives in the water, and from tadpole to adult amphibian, which may live on land, in water, in trees, or elsewhere, depending on the species—is called "metamorphosis."

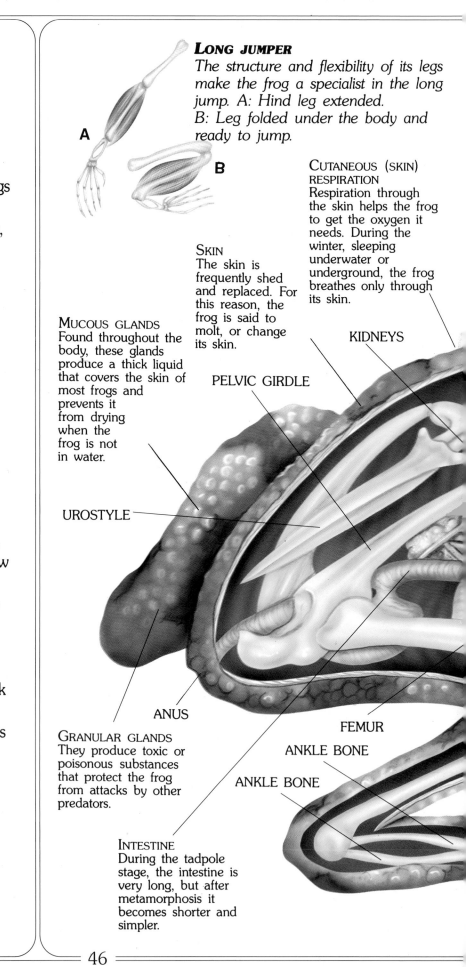

LONG JUMPER
The structure and flexibility of its legs make the frog a specialist in the long jump. A: Hind leg extended.
B: Leg folded under the body and ready to jump.

A

B

CUTANEOUS (SKIN) RESPIRATION
Respiration through the skin helps the frog to get the oxygen it needs. During the winter, sleeping underwater or underground, the frog breathes only through its skin.

SKIN
The skin is frequently shed and replaced. For this reason, the frog is said to molt, or change its skin.

KIDNEYS

PELVIC GIRDLE

MUCOUS GLANDS
Found throughout the body, these glands produce a thick liquid that covers the skin of most frogs and prevents it from drying when the frog is not in water.

UROSTYLE

ANUS

GRANULAR GLANDS
They produce toxic or poisonous substances that protect the frog from attacks by other predators.

FEMUR
ANKLE BONE

ANKLE BONE

INTESTINE
During the tadpole stage, the intestine is very long, but after metamorphosis it becomes shorter and simpler.

THE FROG: LIFE IN TWO WORLDS

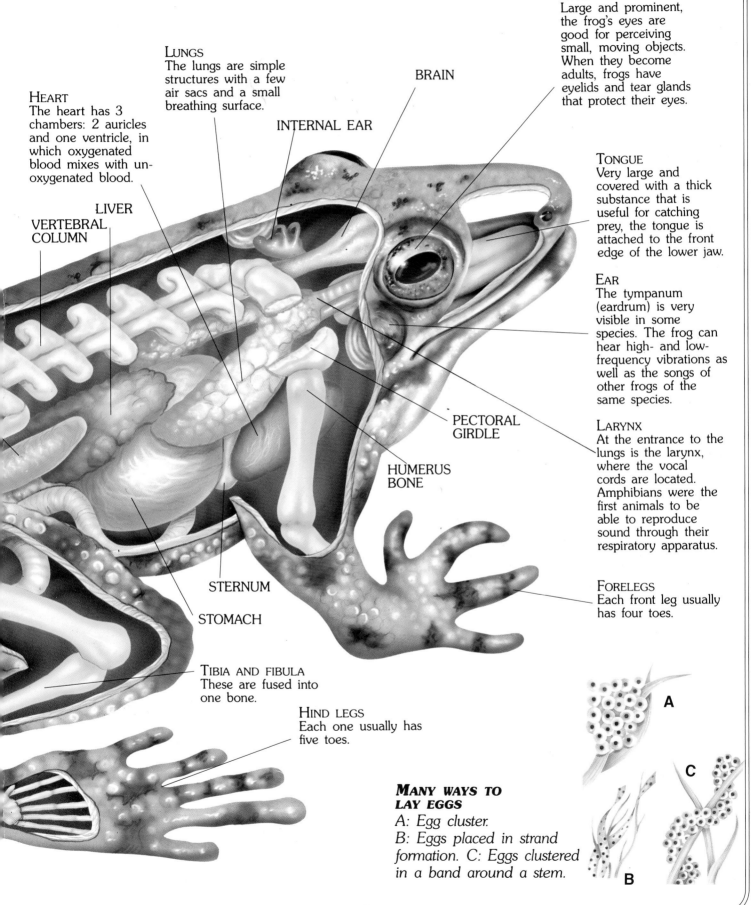

EYES
Large and prominent, the frog's eyes are good for perceiving small, moving objects. When they become adults, frogs have eyelids and tear glands that protect their eyes.

LUNGS
The lungs are simple structures with a few air sacs and a small breathing surface.

BRAIN

HEART
The heart has 3 chambers: 2 auricles and one ventricle, in which oxygenated blood mixes with un-oxygenated blood.

INTERNAL EAR

LIVER
VERTEBRAL COLUMN

TONGUE
Very large and covered with a thick substance that is useful for catching prey, the tongue is attached to the front edge of the lower jaw.

EAR
The tympanum (eardrum) is very visible in some species. The frog can hear high- and low-frequency vibrations as well as the songs of other frogs of the same species.

PECTORAL GIRDLE

LARYNX
At the entrance to the lungs is the larynx, where the vocal cords are located. Amphibians were the first animals to be able to reproduce sound through their respiratory apparatus.

HUMERUS BONE

STERNUM

STOMACH

FORELEGS
Each front leg usually has four toes.

TIBIA AND FIBULA
These are fused into one bone.

HIND LEGS
Each one usually has five toes.

MANY WAYS TO LAY EGGS
A: Egg cluster.
B: Eggs placed in strand formation. C: Eggs clustered in a band around a stem.

A

C

B

THE CROCODILE:

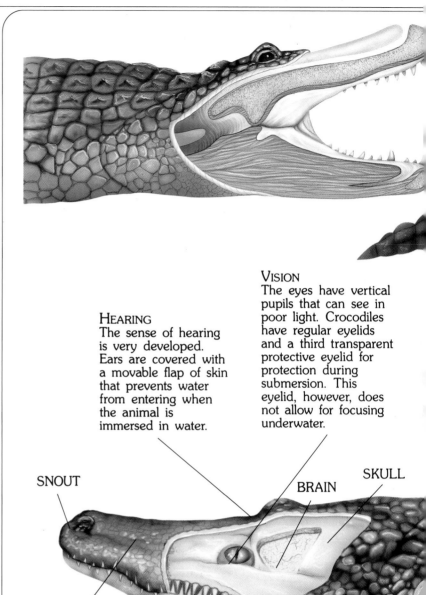

Crocodiles are reptiles that live in water and on land. The crocodile group includes three different families: crocodiles, alligators and gavials (gharials), large reptiles of southern Asia. All have a skeleton made of bone and a body covered with scales. They all are egg-layers.

How they live. The largest and most aggressive crocodiles dominate their neighbors and choose the best places to lay their eggs and search for food. Dominant males defend their territory, especially when they find good food sources.

Egg laying. At breeding time, when the larger male and smaller female meet, they rub their heads and bodies together, make bubbles with their mouths and noses, swim in circles, submerge and re-submerge themselves and make sounds until, at last, they mate. Five or 6 months later, the female digs a nest with her hind legs near a river bank. There, she lays approximately 80 eggs that she packs in and covers with dirt.

During the 85 days the eggs incubate, she will not eat. She remains near the nest to defend it.

When she hears the cries of her young, she digs up the nest, collects the young in her mouth and carries them to the water.

A giant crocodile. The saltwater crocodile is the largest in the world. It can measure up to 20 feet (6m) in length and weigh 2,200 pounds (1,000kg).

HEARING
The sense of hearing is very developed. Ears are covered with a movable flap of skin that prevents water from entering when the animal is immersed in water.

VISION
The eyes have vertical pupils that can see in poor light. Crocodiles have regular eyelids and a third transparent protective eyelid for protection during submersion. This eyelid, however, does not allow for focusing underwater.

SNOUT

BRAIN

SKULL

HOLDING TEETH
These teeth are used to seize and hold prey. Crocodiles often submerge their victims and drown them before swallowing them.

POWERFUL JAWS
Only the lower jaw is movable. The upper jaw remains fixed. This mobility allows the crocodile to gulp down large prey whole or in parts.

ESOPHAGUS

TOOTH REPLACEMENT
All teeth are cone-shaped and can last up to 2 years. Those closer to the end of the snout are replaced more frequently than those near the throat.

SURVIVOR FROM THE PAST

OPENING THE MOUTH UNDERWATER
Crocodiles have a bone in their palate that allows them to eat or grasp their victims and breathe at the same time. They also have a valve that blocks the entrance of water into the throat when their mouth is open underwater.

TEMPERATURE CONTROL
Crocodiles' body temperature depends on the temperature outside. They help to regulate it by basking in the sun or staying longer in the water.

SPINAL COLUMN

BREASTPLATE
Some species of crocodile have bodies totally armored with inner plates of bony skin. Others have fewer or smaller shields and are less protected but more flexible.

STOMACH
Since their teeth are not made for chewing, crocodiles usually swallow their prey in large pieces. Digestion takes place in the stomach, where everything but bones can be digested.

SCALES

PELVIS

LUNG

INTESTINE

FEMUR

HIND LEG

FIBULA

TIBIA

HEART

TRACHEA

BLOOD CIRCULATION
Unlike other reptiles but like mammals and birds, crocodiles have a heart with 4 chambers, which adds to the efficiency of their movements.

PULMONARY RESPIRATION
Crocodiles take in air through nasal openings. A valve situated in the palate separates water from air, allowing the crocodile to breathe and at the same time hold a victim in the water.

49

Chameleons are lizards, a type of reptile whose length varies, according to the species, from 2 inches (5cm) to 2 feet (60cm). They live in the Near East, southern Europe and Africa.

Slowly but surely. The chameleon is an animal of slow movements. It usually takes one step at a time. As it travels from branch to branch, it first moves one front leg very slowly, grabs onto another branch and slowly follows with the other leg.

Looking both ways at once. The chameleon's eyes can move independently of each other. This gives it an unusual capability: it can look in one direction with one eye and in another direction with the other eye, and have perfect command of its surroundings.

Hunting with the tongue. When the chameleon goes hunting, which is almost always, its eyes rotate non-stop, taking in everything around.

The moment an insect comes within reach, the chameleon extends its very long tongue and snares its victim, who adheres to the sticky surface.

Change of color. The chameleon is noted for its ability to change color, hiding from the enemy by blending into the surroundings. It is also able to communicate its state of mind to others of the same species. For example, when angry, chameleons turn black.

LIKE A JELLY ROLL
The tail is rolled up in a circle and can hardly move from side to side. When the chameleon gradually uncurls its tail, it is like unrolling a jelly roll.

SKIN
Not only can the chameleon change color, but, like most reptiles, it can change its skin. The skin is molted and sometimes eaten.

STOMACH

BODY
Viewed from the side, the chameleon's compressed body looks like a leaf on a tree. This thinness helps it to maintain its balance.

INTESTINE

TAIL
The tail is very flexible and is used to grab on to branches. Because of this, it is almost like having a fifth limb. The inside skin has spiny scales so that it can hold on to things more effectively.

HIND FEET
There are also 2 groups of toes on the hind feet: 3 face outside and 2 inside, just the reverse of the forefeet.

CHANGING COLOR

LUNGS
The lungs have many air sacs. These sacs increase the breathing surface, and the chameleon can also inflate them to make it appear larger to its enemies.

ACCELERATOR MUSCLE
The tongue is launched by reflex action. The accelerator muscle in back of the tongue is responsible for this speed.

EYES
Chameleons constantly move their eyes, each one independently. Using this ability, chameleons can see around them almost 360°. This is very important when looking out for prey or predators.

EYELIDS
The chameleon's bulky eyes look like large fortresses. Eyelids are circular with a hole in the center so that the iris can see through.

HEART

LIVER

BRAIN

TRACHEA

TIP OF THE TONGUE
The tip of the tongue can pick up food items the way the trunk of an elephant can.

TONGUE
After spotting an insect, the chameleon extends its long tongue with fantastic speed. The poor insect has no chance of escape.

HEAD
The chameleon's head is like a helmet equipped with one or more horns. These adornments enable chameleons to recognize each other and to stand out in combat.

FOREFEET
For grabbing on to branches, chameleons have five toes with strong claws: 2 toes turned to the outside and 3 toes turned toward the inside.

SHOULDER
Shoulder and hip joints are very flexible, allowing the chameleon to move its limbs to any nearby branch.

DRAWING CLOSE TO FOOD
The chameleon has a very specialized tongue. Long and flexible, it is also prehensile—able to wrap itself around objects. It can snare insects that are surprisingly far away.

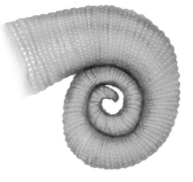

THE SNAKE:

Snakes are reptiles, but they are very different from most other animals in this group, such as crocodiles, lizards and turtles. Part of the difference lies in their narrow, long and legless bodies. But there is much more.

Smelling with the tongue. In order to follow the trail of its prey, a snake is led by smell and the heat given off by the prey. To smell, the snake extends its tongue and then places the forks of the tongue in its nostrils, which are located in the palate.

Swallowing victims whole. When snakes detect their prey, many species snare it by using their teeth. The teeth are used to immobilize the victim, but not for chewing. The prey must be swallowed whole. This can be done even with prey twice the size of the snake's head, because of the snake's very flexible jaws and its movable ribs that allow the prey to pass through.

Dangerous snakes. Only about 500 of the 2,500 known species of snakes are dangerous to humans. Of these, the poisonous ones are not the only danger. Large snakes, like the boa constrictor and python, can kill by wrapping themselves around their victims and squeezing until the prey chokes or loses consciousness and is devoured.

Some poisonous snakes can inject venom from their hollow fangs. One poisonous snake is the rattlesnake, which got its name from the sound made by the rattle on its tail when the snake is disturbed.

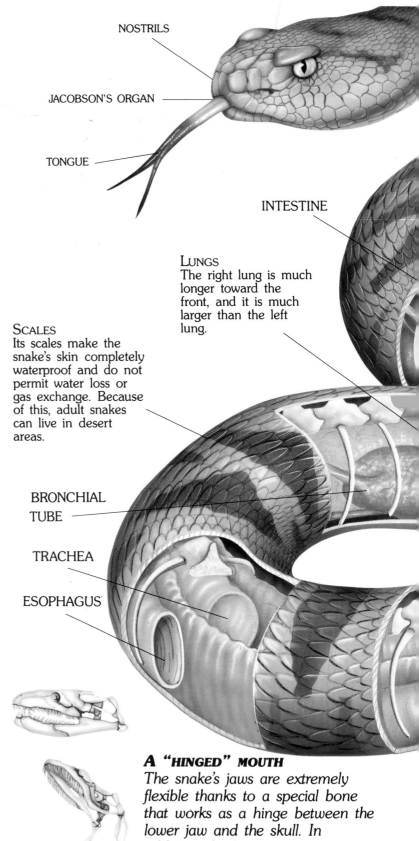

NOSTRILS

JACOBSON'S ORGAN

TONGUE

INTESTINE

LUNGS
The right lung is much longer toward the front, and it is much larger than the left lung.

SCALES
Its scales make the snake's skin completely waterproof and do not permit water loss or gas exchange. Because of this, adult snakes can live in desert areas.

BRONCHIAL TUBE

TRACHEA

ESOPHAGUS

A "HINGED" MOUTH
The snake's jaws are extremely flexible thanks to a special bone that works as a hinge between the lower jaw and the skull. In addition, the lower jaw can expand on either side through an elastic ligament situated on the chin.

SWALLOWING WITHOUT CHEWING

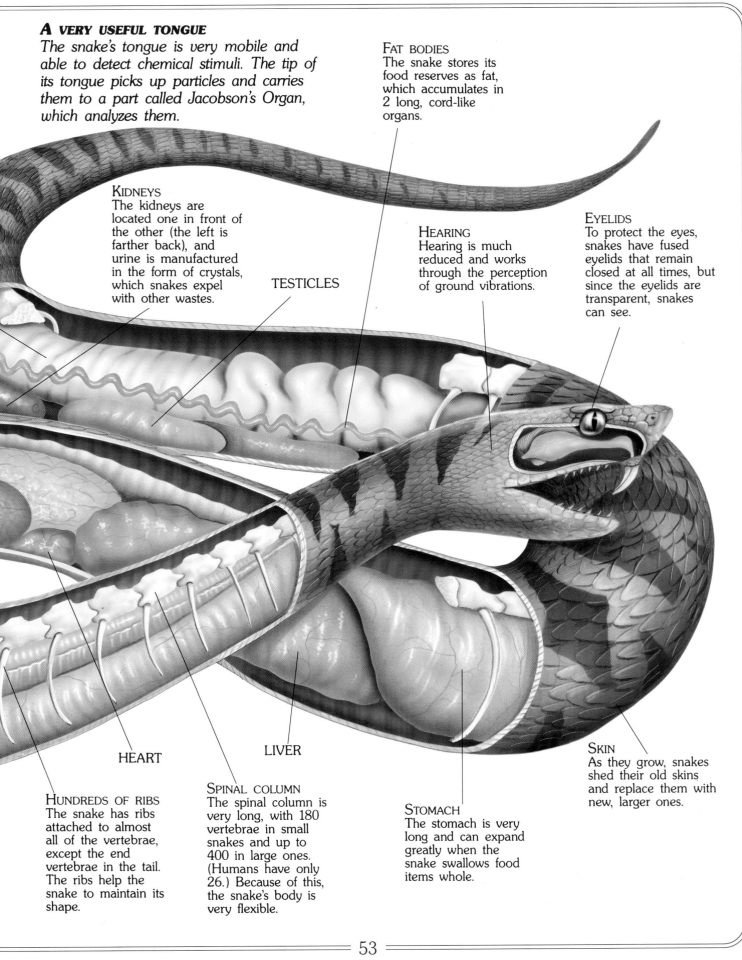

A VERY USEFUL TONGUE

The snake's tongue is very mobile and able to detect chemical stimuli. The tip of its tongue picks up particles and carries them to a part called Jacobson's Organ, which analyzes them.

FAT BODIES
The snake stores its food reserves as fat, which accumulates in 2 long, cord-like organs.

KIDNEYS
The kidneys are located one in front of the other (the left is farther back), and urine is manufactured in the form of crystals, which snakes expel with other wastes.

TESTICLES

HEARING is much reduced and works through the perception of ground vibrations.

EYELIDS
To protect the eyes, snakes have fused eyelids that remain closed at all times, but since the eyelids are transparent, snakes can see.

HEART

LIVER

HUNDREDS OF RIBS
The snake has ribs attached to almost all of the vertebrae, except the end vertebrae in the tail. The ribs help the snake to maintain its shape.

SPINAL COLUMN
The spinal column is very long, with 180 vertebrae in small snakes and up to 400 in large ones. (Humans have only 26.) Because of this, the snake's body is very flexible.

STOMACH
The stomach is very long and can expand greatly when the snake swallows food items whole.

SKIN
As they grow, snakes shed their old skins and replace them with new, larger ones.

Birds

There are almost 10,000 species of birds in the world and they
come in a wide variety of sizes, from the tiny bee hummingbird
to the large ostrich, which is nearly 10 feet (3m) high. There are
also a fantastic variety of life forms and behavior. Some birds
cannot fly, and others are capable of flying thousands of miles.
Birds of prey can reach speeds of more than 155 miles (250km)
an hour when making their dizzying downward dives.

Birds are nature's perfect flying machines. Their bones are light and hollow; they have sacs filled with air inside their bodies; and they have wings and strong muscles to move them.

The mating dance. When the time comes to reproduce, males court females by showing off their beautiful feathers, singing songs and even offering gifts, such as plants.

There are spectacular courtships: the peacock unfolds his tail feathers; the frigate bird blows up his flashy red crop; and the bird of paradise hangs upside down like an acrobat to impress the female.

Types of flight. Almost all birds can fly, and many forms of flight exist.

The albatross, for example, can glide for thousands of miles without flapping its wings. The kestrel flies without moving its wings by using currents in the air. And the hummingbird can hover immobile in the air by beating its wings at great speed, up to 80 beats per second. Most birds, however, flap their wings, taking advantage of air currents.

The smallest bird. The world's smallest bird is the bee hummingbird of Cuba, measuring 2 inches (5cm) in length and weighing one-eighteenth of an ounce.

The largest bird. The largest non-flying bird is the ostrich. The male can reach almost 10 feet (3m) in height and weigh more than 330 pounds (150kg).

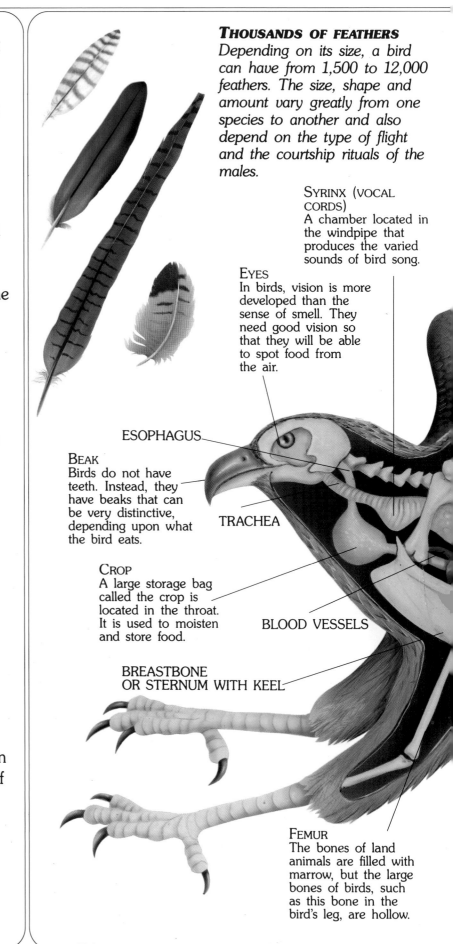

THOUSANDS OF FEATHERS
Depending on its size, a bird can have from 1,500 to 12,000 feathers. The size, shape and amount vary greatly from one species to another and also depend on the type of flight and the courtship rituals of the males.

SYRINX (VOCAL CORDS)
A chamber located in the windpipe that produces the varied sounds of bird song.

EYES
In birds, vision is more developed than the sense of smell. They need good vision so that they will be able to spot food from the air.

ESOPHAGUS

BEAK
Birds do not have teeth. Instead, they have beaks that can be very distinctive, depending upon what the bird eats.

TRACHEA

CROP
A large storage bag called the crop is located in the throat. It is used to moisten and store food.

BLOOD VESSELS

BREASTBONE OR STERNUM WITH KEEL

FEMUR
The bones of land animals are filled with marrow, but the large bones of birds, such as this bone in the bird's leg, are hollow.

BIRDS: OWNERS OF THE AIR

How they fly
The shape of the wing determines how much "lift" the air will give in flight; most birds flap their wings to produce lift.

OVARY
The ovary is the female reproductive organ. Most vertebrate animals have 2, one on the left and another on the right, but because weight is a factor, birds have only one ovary.

GIZZARD
Equivalent to part of the stomach of other animals, the gizzard works as a grinder. It is useful for crushing the grains that birds eat.

KIDNEY
Birds do not produce urine like mammals, but a semi-solid white substance called guano, to save water.

EGGSHELL GLAND
Females need this gland to produce the shell of the egg.

AIR SACS
These sacs of air help to make birds lighter and cooler. They pass air in and out of the lungs.

PELVIS

INTESTINE

LIVER

HEART
The bird's heart is larger than that of a mammal of the same size. A canary's heart beats 514 times per minute, and a hummingbird's beats 615 times per minute. But heart rate is related to body size. A human's heart beats 72 times a minute.

CLOACA
This is the end of the intestine. It also receives ducts from the ovary and kidney.

All birds are oviparous. That means the females lay eggs with embryos inside that may later develop into chicks.

Laying eggs. Courtship rituals allow the male and female to "get to know each other." If the female accepts her suitor, they mate. That means they join their sexual organs, called cloacas. An embryo begins to form inside the egg inside the body of the female. But before the embryo reaches a weight that would slow down the flight of the mother, she will lay the egg.

Birth of the chick. It is generally the female who takes care of the *incubation* of the eggs, covering them with her body and keeping them warm so that the chicks will grow inside them.

Some time later, the chicks will completely develop and be ready to leave the eggs. This will be a tremendous effort for the chick, because it has to break the shell from inside by hitting it with a tooth located in its beak. Most chicks, however, accomplish this task in less than half an hour.

The color of the eggs varies from the white eggs of owls to the blue-and-green eggs of the grey heron. Shapes also vary: there are eggs with sharp-pointed ends like the grebe's (a species of wild duck), and eggs in the shape of a spinning top, like those of the shore bird, or curlew.

AT THE START OF DEVELOPMENT

YOLK
The yolk that feeds the chick contains vitamins, fats, proteins and mineral salts. Sometimes eggs without yolks appear. This is the result of a flaw in which the shell has formed around a bit of tissue instead of an embryo.

AIR CHAMBER
Without an air chamber in which oxygen can be stored, the chick would die inside the egg. The chick will breathe air from this chamber through its lungs just before hatching.

WHITE OF THE EGG (ALBUMIN)

EMBRYO

STRANDS OF ALBUMIN

EGGSHELL
Although it may appear smooth, the shell has many pores through which air passes, allowing the chick to absorb oxygen from the outside. The thickness of the shell depends on the species. The eggshell of an ostrich weighs 3¼ pounds (1.5kg) and measures ½ inch (2mm) thick.

FEATHERS
Here the chick is wet, but within a few hours, this hen chick will be covered with a dry, brilliant yellow down to keep it warm. Although this chick will not fly at once, some chicks can do so 15 days after hatching!

GREY HERON EGG

CURLEW EGG

GREBE EGG

TAWNY OWL EGG

A WIDE VARIETY
The shape, size and color of the egg varies greatly from one species to another. Here are 4 examples.

THE CHICK: LEAVING THE EGG

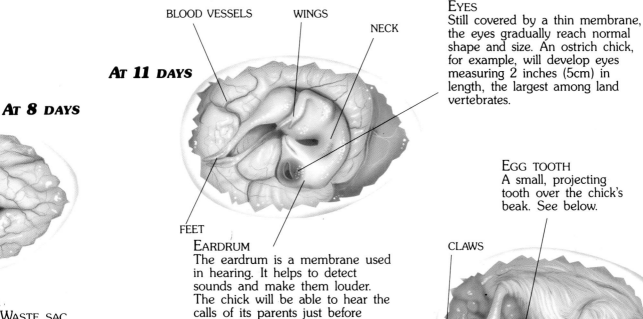

AT 8 DAYS

AT 11 DAYS

BLOOD VESSELS WINGS NECK

FEET

EYES
Still covered by a thin membrane, the eyes gradually reach normal shape and size. An ostrich chick, for example, will develop eyes measuring 2 inches (5cm) in length, the largest among land vertebrates.

EGG TOOTH
A small, projecting tooth over the chick's beak. See below.

CLAWS

EARDRUM
The eardrum is a membrane used in hearing. It helps to detect sounds and make them louder. The chick will be able to hear the calls of its parents just before leaving the egg.

WASTE SAC
This sac contains the chick's wastes, which remain inside the egg.

AT 15 DAYS

NOSTRILS
A few hours before hatching, the chick's nostrils will open up and the chicken will breathe with its lungs for the first time. Up to this point, it has absorbed air through the eggshell via the yolk and blood vessels.

AT 20 DAYS

FEET
At 20 days of development, the chick's feet are completely formed and visible with scales and claws, well prepared for life on the ground rather than in flight.

EGG TOOTH
Chicks break the shell with a special tooth they have on their beak. A short time after birth, when no longer needed, the tooth falls out.

Storks are large, majestic birds that live near marshes and wetlands. There are 17 species that live all over the world except in extremely cold places.

An awkward bird. The stork has a large bill, a long neck and especially large feet. Its feathers are usually black and white. Storks almost always live near water, and they nest in trees or on cliffs or on the roofs of houses.

Bird migrations. The stork, like many other species of bird, travels thousands of miles twice each year. It leaves the place where its young were born and raised, flies to another location for the winter, and returns home the following spring. These yearly journeys are called migrations. The stork travels more than 6,000 miles (10,000km) away from home— one way—to spend the winter and then flies 6,000 miles back.

See you at home. Male and female storks return to the same nest year after year. Their courtship consists of "saying hello" with a noisy opening and closing of their bills. After they mate, the female will lay from 6 to 8 eggs that both mother and father stork keep warm for 30 days.

Not all of the chicks, however, are born at the same time. In this way, nature makes sure that in times of scarcity, some chicks will survive.

A VERY SPECIALIZED BILL

Most storks have a large, perfectly straight bill. There is one stork, though, that has a very odd bill: it's the Open-billed Stork, whose bill does not completely close but leaves a space large enough to hold mussels and snails. Using the sharp edges of its bill, the stork then cuts the muscles that keep the mussel shells closed.

PLUMAGE
The species of stork with the widest range is the Common Stork. It measures 3 feet (90cm) high with mostly white feathers, except for some black flight feathers. Its bill and large feet are red.

RADIUS AND ULNA

HUMERUS

RIBS

EYES
Generally, birds have good vision, but scientists believe that migratory birds have a special organ near the retina (the screen in back of their eyes) that can determine the location of the sun.

NECK

BILL
The stork's bill is straight, long and heavy. The stork uses it to capture fish, frogs and insects. When males and females greet each other in their nest, they usually make a clacking sound with their bills.

BRAIN
No one knows what guides birds during migrations. They do seem to have some kind of map of the sky and a way of knowing the hour of the day and the season of the year.

THE STORK: ITS MIGRATION

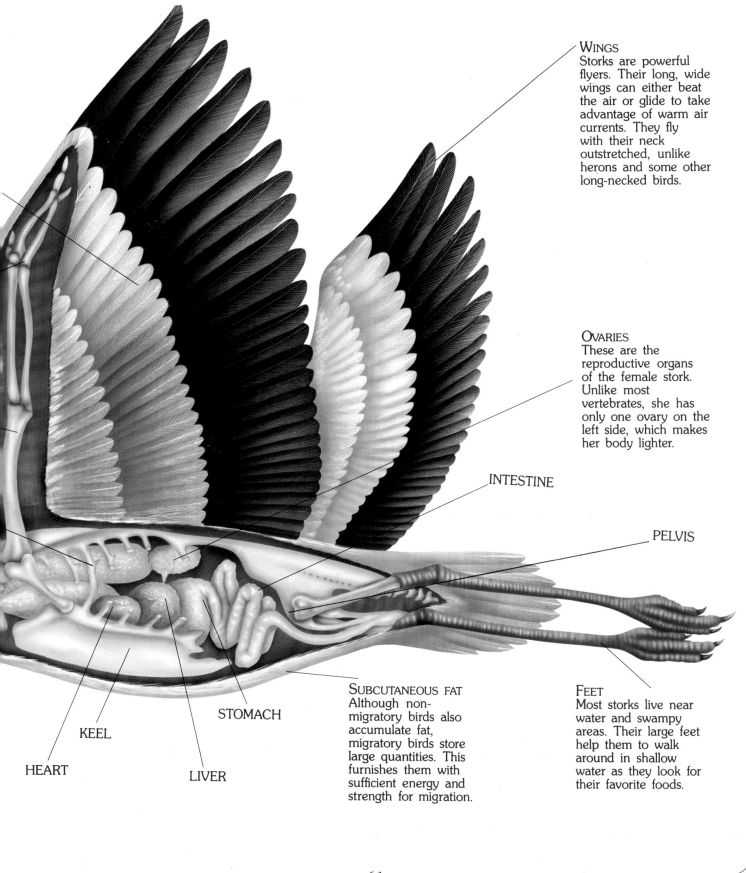

WINGS
Storks are powerful flyers. Their long, wide wings can either beat the air or glide to take advantage of warm air currents. They fly with their neck outstretched, unlike herons and some other long-necked birds.

OVARIES
These are the reproductive organs of the female stork. Unlike most vertebrates, she has only one ovary on the left side, which makes her body lighter.

INTESTINE

PELVIS

SUBCUTANEOUS FAT
Although non-migratory birds also accumulate fat, migratory birds store large quantities. This furnishes them with sufficient energy and strength for migration.

FEET
Most storks live near water and swampy areas. Their large feet help them to walk around in shallow water as they look for their favorite foods.

STOMACH

KEEL

HEART

LIVER

Mammals

These features are characteristic of mammals: they are covered with hair, and the females feed the young with milk from the mother. Mammals are classified into three groups: the monotremes, a group of egg-laying mammals that includes the platypus and echidna; the marsupials, including the kangaroo and koala, whose young develop after birth in the female's pouch, and the placentals. In the last group, we include humans and all other mammals. The females have a placenta, which is connected to the unborn baby, providing oxygen and food. The young are well formed when they are born.

Moles are insect-eating mammals that are usually about the size of a rat. The common mole lives in the fields and gardens of Europe and Asia. The star-nosed mole has a peculiar nose with tentacles on it. It lives in wet, swampy land in North America.

A tireless digger. The common mole is a champion digger that can build a system of very complicated underground passages. Working with its paws, it pushes and piles up earth toward the outside of a new or unused tunnel.

An underground maze. The mole's dwelling consists of a nest and a large chamber with grass and straw. There is also a storage area of earthworms, a mole's favorite winter food, and hunting passages with large tunnels leading to an exit through holes called "molehills."

Hunting underground. When earthworms or other invertebrates that live underground fall into one of the hunting tunnels, the mole, out on patrol, is quick to make a meal of them.

If the ground is not rich in food, moles can travel and dig up to 330 feet (100m) from the central chamber or nest to find more food.

Good swimmers. Among moles, the star-nosed mole is the best swimmer. In winter, it digs in the snow and can swim under the ice formed on rivers and lakes.

MINERS OF THE DEPTHS
As moles construct deep tunnels, they become "living wagons" carrying earth to the surface. Near the surface, they push up the earth and form small hills.

SKIN
The mole's skin is thick, more so around the chest area, since the chest supports the weight of the animal when it is digging and resting.

FUR

BODY
The mole's body is compact, with a very short neck. Its shape is well suited for travelling through narrow tunnels in which, although it is hard to believe, moles can turn around.

INTESTINE

FEMUR

TAIL
In common moles, the tail is used for touch and is held straight out, especially when the mole is moving backwards.

FEET
The feet are used more as an anchor inside the tunnels than for actual digging.

THE MOLE: LIVING UNDERGROUND

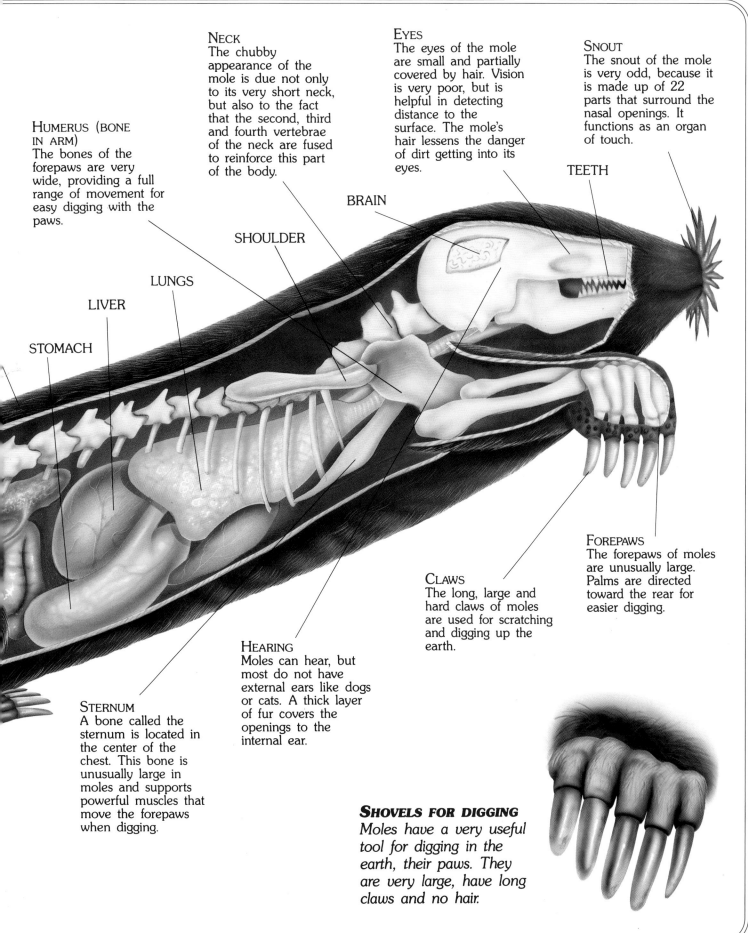

NECK
The chubby appearance of the mole is due not only to its very short neck, but also to the fact that the second, third and fourth vertebrae of the neck are fused to reinforce this part of the body.

EYES
The eyes of the mole are small and partially covered by hair. Vision is very poor, but is helpful in detecting distance to the surface. The mole's hair lessens the danger of dirt getting into its eyes.

SNOUT
The snout of the mole is very odd, because it is made up of 22 parts that surround the nasal openings. It functions as an organ of touch.

HUMERUS (BONE IN ARM)
The bones of the forepaws are very wide, providing a full range of movement for easy digging with the paws.

TEETH

BRAIN

SHOULDER

LUNGS

LIVER

STOMACH

FOREPAWS
The forepaws of moles are unusually large. Palms are directed toward the rear for easier digging.

CLAWS
The long, large and hard claws of moles are used for scratching and digging up the earth.

HEARING
Moles can hear, but most do not have external ears like dogs or cats. A thick layer of fur covers the openings to the internal ear.

STERNUM
A bone called the sternum is located in the center of the chest. This bone is unusually large in moles and supports powerful muscles that move the forepaws when digging.

SHOVELS FOR DIGGING
Moles have a very useful tool for digging in the earth, their paws. They are very large, have long claws and no hair.

The beaver is one of the largest rodents, about 3 feet (1m) in length. There are only two species: the European beaver, found only in the Scandinavian countries and in parts of Russia and France, and the North American beaver that lives in Canada and northern parts of the United States.

An able swimmer. The hind feet are webbed like those of a duck, which makes the beaver an excellent swimmer. Its tail acts as a rudder.

When the beaver goes underwater, its nostrils and ears seal completely. This allows it to remain underwater while filling its "warehouse of wood" in the river bed. This warehouse is like a food pantry where tree bark, which the beaver eats, is stored. It is also a place to warehouse branches and tree trunks.

A house on the water. A beaver's lodge is located along the banks of a river or at the center of a dam that the beaver has constructed. The lodge is made by accumulating large quantities of sticks and branches in the river bed in an enormous pile. When the lodge is finished, the beaver gnaws away at the wood to open an underwater entrance.

Dam builder. Beaver dams can measure 6½ feet (2m) high and up to 330 feet (100m) long. Many of them are formed with sticks fastened to the bottom of the river, which in turn are secured to other sticks. Tree trunks are placed horizontally.

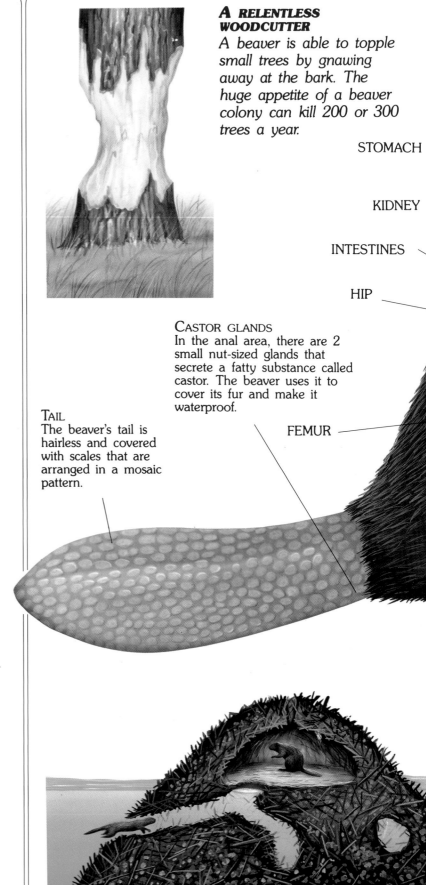

A RELENTLESS WOODCUTTER
A beaver is able to topple small trees by gnawing away at the bark. The huge appetite of a beaver colony can kill 200 or 300 trees a year.

STOMACH

KIDNEY

INTESTINES

HIP

CASTOR GLANDS
In the anal area, there are 2 small nut-sized glands that secrete a fatty substance called castor. The beaver uses it to cover its fur and make it waterproof.

FEMUR

TAIL
The beaver's tail is hairless and covered with scales that are arranged in a mosaic pattern.

THE BEAVER ARCHITECT

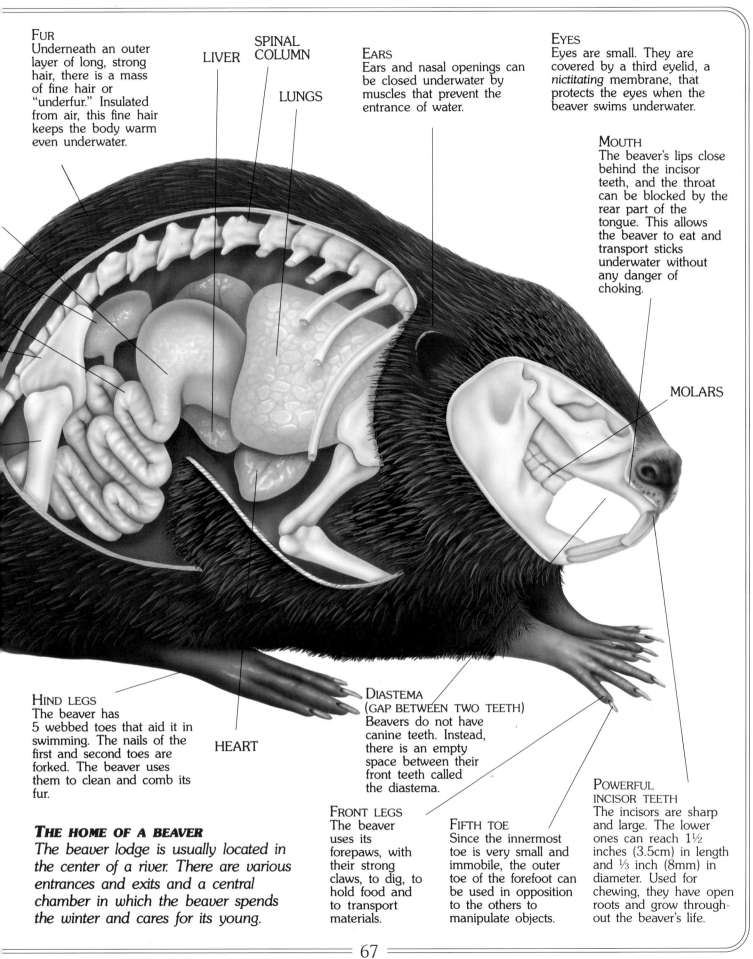

FUR
Underneath an outer layer of long, strong hair, there is a mass of fine hair or "underfur." Insulated from air, this fine hair keeps the body warm even underwater.

LIVER

SPINAL COLUMN

LUNGS

EARS
Ears and nasal openings can be closed underwater by muscles that prevent the entrance of water.

EYES
Eyes are small. They are covered by a third eyelid, a *nictitating* membrane, that protects the *eyes* when the beaver swims underwater.

MOUTH
The beaver's lips close behind the incisor teeth, and the throat can be blocked by the rear part of the tongue. This allows the beaver to eat and transport sticks underwater without any danger of choking.

MOLARS

HIND LEGS
The beaver has 5 webbed toes that aid it in swimming. The nails of the first and second toes are forked. The beaver uses them to clean and comb its fur.

HEART

DIASTEMA
(GAP BETWEEN TWO TEETH)
Beavers do not have canine teeth. Instead, there is an empty space between their front teeth called the diastema.

FRONT LEGS
The beaver uses its forepaws, with their strong claws, to dig, to hold food and to transport materials.

FIFTH TOE
Since the innermost toe is very small and immobile, the outer toe of the forefoot can be used in opposition to the others to manipulate objects.

POWERFUL INCISOR TEETH
The incisors are sharp and large. The lower ones can reach 1½ inches (3.5cm) in length and ⅓ inch (8mm) in diameter. Used for chewing, they have open roots and grow throughout the beaver's life.

THE HOME OF A BEAVER
The beaver lodge is usually located in the center of a river. There are various entrances and exits and a central chamber in which the beaver spends the winter and cares for its young.

The basic feature that distinguishes bats from other mammals is their ability to fly. Aside from rodents, they have the most numerous species. Of 4,000 species of mammal, almost 1,000 are bats!

Two large groups. Bats are classified into 2 groups: the *Megachiroptera*, which are fruit-eaters and use vision to get around; and the *Microchiroptera*, which eat lots of different foods (many are insect-eaters) and use echolocation.

Flying in the dark. Microchiropteran bats fly by a system of sound-wave emissions called *echolocation*, a kind of radar. They produce high-frequency sounds in the larynx (voice box), and when these sounds collide with an object—prey, for example—they bounce off and return to the bat. The bat picks up the returning sound waves with its large ears. Within a tenth of a second, the bat's brain has translated the information and now knows what object is in front of it, its location, if it is moving, its direction and speed.

Sleeping during winter. When winter arrives, some types of bat will hang by their feet from racks in the roofs of caves or in tree hollows. They will spend the whole winter there, almost immobile. Meanwhile, their body temperature falls to 41°F (5°C), and they can stop breathing for almost 10 minutes before starting again. They eat nothing. This uses a minimum amount of energy.

A BUTTERFLY NET
A bat's wings can swoop down over many flying insects like a butterfly net.

EARS
The bat's ears are like giant, directional funnels that pick up sound waves bouncing off objects. They can tell whether a space is large enough to enter.

BRAIN
The part of the brain that deals with the outer world through a type of radar is the most developed. Echos picked up by the bat let it know what's out there and where it is.

CLAW
The only finger of the bat's hand that has a claw is the thumb. It is used for climbing, scratching and for holding food. Megachiropterans also use it to swing from branch to branch and as a fastener, when a mother carries her young.

TRACHEA

TRAGUS
The function of this fleshy projection at the entrance to the ear of many bats is to concentrate incoming sounds. Its shape varies among the species.

DUCTS AND NASAL OPENINGS
The twisted shape of the nasal ducts increases the volume of the sounds coming out of the larynx. Coming through the nasal opening, these sounds are directed forward.

THE BAT: FLYING BY RADAR

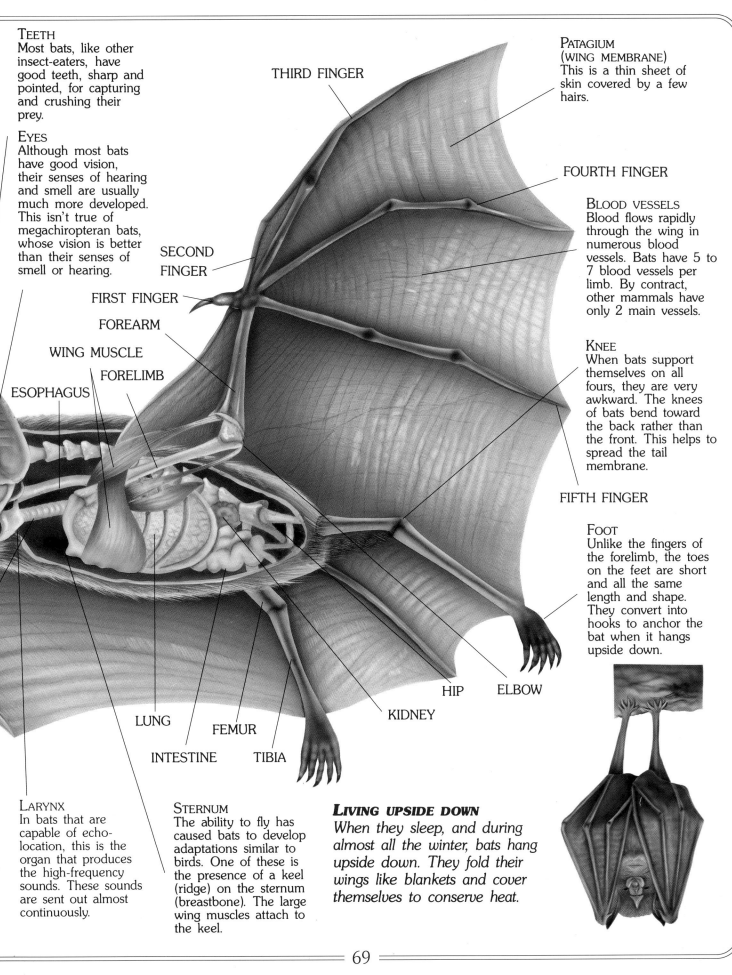

TEETH
Most bats, like other insect-eaters, have good teeth, sharp and pointed, for capturing and crushing their prey.

EYES
Although most bats have good vision, their senses of hearing and smell are usually much more developed. This isn't true of megachiropteran bats, whose vision is better than their senses of smell or hearing.

SECOND FINGER

FIRST FINGER

FOREARM

WING MUSCLE

FORELIMB

ESOPHAGUS

THIRD FINGER

PATAGIUM
(WING MEMBRANE)
This is a thin sheet of skin covered by a few hairs.

FOURTH FINGER

BLOOD VESSELS
Blood flows rapidly through the wing in numerous blood vessels. Bats have 5 to 7 blood vessels per limb. By contract, other mammals have only 2 main vessels.

KNEE
When bats support themselves on all fours, they are very awkward. The knees of bats bend toward the back rather than the front. This helps to spread the tail membrane.

FIFTH FINGER

FOOT
Unlike the fingers of the forelimb, the toes on the feet are short and all the same length and shape. They convert into hooks to anchor the bat when it hangs upside down.

HIP   ELBOW

KIDNEY

LUNG

FEMUR

INTESTINE   TIBIA

LARYNX
In bats that are capable of echo-location, this is the organ that produces the high-frequency sounds. These sounds are sent out almost continuously.

STERNUM
The ability to fly has caused bats to develop adaptations similar to birds. One of these is the presence of a keel (ridge) on the sternum (breastbone). The large wing muscles attach to the keel.

LIVING UPSIDE DOWN
When they sleep, and during almost all the winter, bats hang upside down. They fold their wings like blankets and cover themselves to conserve heat.

Cheetahs are meat-eating mammals that belong to the cat family, or *Felidae*. They live only in Africa and the Near East in savannah areas where they can easily spot their prey and run after it at great speed.

Champion at 100 meters. The body of the cheetah is well designed for short, fast runs. It is sleek and aerodynamic, with long, thin legs.

Like a sports car, cheetahs have great acceleration power. In only 165 feet (50m), they can reach a top speed of 70 miles (115km) per hour.

Cunning and speed. When the cheetah finds prey, it will hide and watch every movement while preparing to attack. At the moment the cheetah gets the advantage, it will tense its muscles, calculate the distance and chase its prey with lightning speed. The cheetah then lunges at the prey and sinks its teeth into the neck.

Learning to hunt. Male and female cheetahs do not live together; they meet only to reproduce. After mating, female cheetahs return to living alone. When it is time to give birth, they move to hidden lairs, where they have from one to 4 cubs.

The mother is in charge of caring for and feeding the cubs and changing lairs from time to time. She also teaches them how to hunt. She captures small live prey, like hares or young gazelles, and then frees them so that her cubs can catch them.

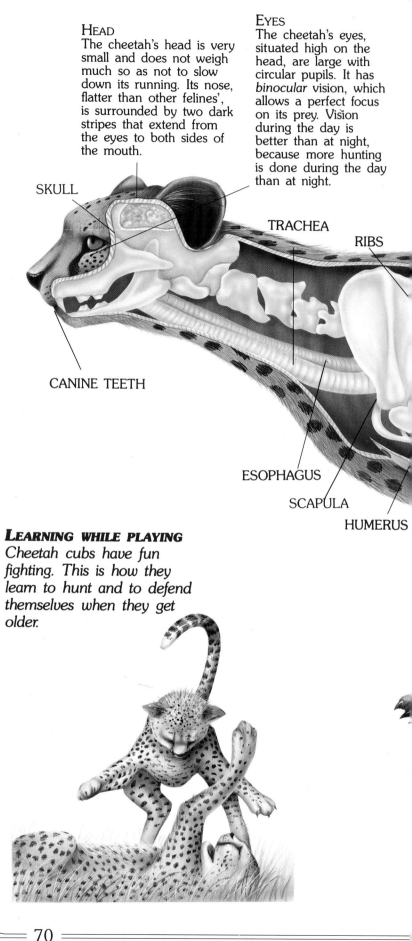

HEAD
The cheetah's head is very small and does not weigh much so as not to slow down its running. Its nose, flatter than other felines', is surrounded by two dark stripes that extend from the eyes to both sides of the mouth.

EYES
The cheetah's eyes, situated high on the head, are large with circular pupils. It has *binocular* vision, which allows a perfect focus on its prey. Vision during the day is better than at night, because more hunting is done during the day than at night.

SKULL

CANINE TEETH

TRACHEA

RIBS

ESOPHAGUS

SCAPULA

HUMERUS

LEARNING WHILE PLAYING
Cheetah cubs have fun fighting. This is how they learn to hunt and to defend themselves when they get older.

THE CHEETAH: FASTEST OF ALL

LUNGS
Like sprinters when given the green light, cheetahs start with great force and reach top speed within a few meters. Their lungs can breathe in and out quickly, from 60 to 150 respirations per minute.

SPINAL COLUMN
At rest, the cheetah's spinal column is straighter than in other felines, but in a full run, the animal has great elasticity. It curves and stretches with each stride. Sometimes it seems to be made of rubber.

SHAPE OF THE BODY
Judging by its silhouette, the cheetah may seem like a thin, weak animal, but in fact, its muscle system is very powerful. The muscles are surrounded by reserves of blood that provide plenty of energy for long runs.

TAIL
The cheetah's tail is longer than half its body and helps to maintain balance while the cheetah is running at great speed. The end is white and has from one to 3 rings instead of round spots.

LIVER

VERTEBRAE

STOMACH

HIP

LEGS
The bones of the cheetah's legs are long and thin so it can achieve a longer stride. The musculature is reduced toward the lower part of the legs, but it is very powerful higher up, which enables the legs to move very rapidly.

TIBIA AND FIBULA

FEMUR

CLAWS
The cheetah's claws are shorter and less curved than other cats'.

HEART
Like the cheetah's other organs, the heart is larger than in other felines, so that more blood is pumped through the body.

PAWS
Cheetahs and many other fast mammals are "digitigrade." That means that when they stand upright only their toes touch the ground. This helps them to run faster.

AN OBSERVATION POST
Good hunters, like the cheetah, need to have their hunting territory under control. The cheetah usually climbs up on a tree trunk or rock to get a panoramic view and observe the movements of its prey.

APES & MONKEYS:

Apes and monkeys are primates, belonging to the same order as humans. There are 4 types of apes: the orangutan and the gibbon that live in Asia, and the chimpanzee and gorilla that live in Africa.

Like our family. Apes are the animals that seem most like human beings. For this reason, they are known as "anthropoids," meaning "similar to humans." They are not, however, our ancestors, but relatives of a common ancestor.

The orangutan. Orangutans measure approximately 4 feet (1.3m) high when standing erect. Normally, they walk on all 4 legs, although they are often seen swinging from trees. Despite their size, they can sleep in nests among the treetops.

The gibbon. This is the smallest member of the ape group. Gibbons are accustomed to living in families.

The chimpanzee. This ape has the level of intelligence closest to humans'. Chimpanzees can, for example, make use of sticks to extract honey from honeycombs or chew leaves to form a sponge with which to soak up water deposited in tree hollows.

The gorilla. This is the largest of the apes. Some males exceed 6 feet (1.8m) in height and their weight varies from 400 to 440 pounds (180–200kg).

SPIDER MONKEYS
Some monkeys have very long tails and limbs that provide balance when moving from branch to branch among the treetops.

KIDNEY

TAIL
Mandrills (baboons) have a short tail and often hold it erect so that their young, which they carry on their back, will not fall off. They also use their tail to express their moods.

INTESTINE

CALLUS
(HARDENED SKIN)
On their buttocks, baboons have hairless areas in brilliant colors. These areas are more pronounced in males than in females.

FORWARD-FACING EYES
With movable and flexible forelimbs, primates are able to handle objects directly before their eyes.

RELATIVES OF HUMANS

BABOON (MANDRILL)

CHEEK POUCHES
Baboons have pouches in their cheeks for accumulating food; these pouches can hold almost as much as their stomach can.

SHOULDER

TEETH
Like humans, baboons have 32 teeth, but they retain powerful canine teeth, especially the males. Canine teeth in humans are much smaller.

BRAIN
The larger size of the brain in primates makes complex behavior possible. It also means they have a greater capacity for learning than other animals, and at a faster rate.

EARS
The ears of baboons are small, pointed and scarcely movable. However, some monkeys, because of their muscle system, can point their ears toward the source of a sound.

EYES
Primates have eyes shifted forward, not sideways, as in many other mammals. Some can even see colors, which helps them obtain more information about their surroundings.

NOSE
For most land mammals, the senses of smell and hearing are vital for survival. Survival is possible for a monkey without the sense of smell, but a blind one has little chance.

LUNGS

STOMACH

HEART

BODY
In most primates, the skin is covered with hair except for the palms of the forelimbs and soles of the feet. Our ancestors also wore this "fur."

FORELIMBS
The forelimbs of primates are among the most specialized in the animal kingdom. With them, they can grasp, pick up objects, and clean up after themselves—and do many other things that humans know how to do with their hands!

FACE
Baboons are the most colorful monkeys. The nose is red and surrounded by small wrinkled blue sacs. These colors stand out more in the male, which also has a yellow beard.

TOENAILS
Toes of primates do not have claws but flat nails. Many use their forelimbs to put food in their mouths or pick up their young.

UPPER JAW

LOWER JAW

THE BEAR:

Although bears will eat almost anything, they are classified as carnivores, which means "meat-eaters." There are 8 species, including very large bears like the polar bear; brown bear; grizzly; and black bear. The remaining species are smaller: the sloth bear; the ucumari, or spectacled bear; Malay, or sun bear; and Asiatic black bear.

Four months without eating. Some species of bear, like other animals that live in cold climates, have developed a system of survival for the winter. This is called hibernation and it means sleeping during the winter months, while many bodily functions including heartbeat, frequency of respiration, and temperature are reduced to save energy.

Before winter arrives, however, bears eat as much as they can. From this food, they will obtain the low amount of energy needed during the winter.

The largest bear. The Kodiak bear is a relative of the polar bear. At 10 feet (3m) in height and weighing 1,800 pounds (800kg), the Kodiak along with the polar bear are the largest land meat-eaters in existence. Kodiak bears live on Kodiak, an island off the coast of Alaska.

A great swimmer. Of all bears, the best swimmer is the polar bear. Polar bears can swim non-stop across distances of more than 6 miles (10km). They swim by using their forepaws as oars.

SLEEPING ALL WINTER
The polar bear spends all winter sleeping to conserve energy. The newborn bear cubs must suckle alone.

KIDNEY

INTESTINES

HIP

SKIN
If bears got their skin wet while swimming underwater, they would freeze to death in cold polar waters. They don't, because between their skin and fur is a layer of soft, waterproof hair called underfur. This layer traps air and keeps the bear warm and dry.

URINARY BLADDER

FEMUR

AN INSULATING LAYER
Bears have a thick layer of fat under the skin. By the time winter comes, they have accumulated great reserves of fat, thickening this layer even more as a protection from the cold. This fat also provides nutrients that the bear uses when it hibernates.

TIBIA

BONES OF THE FEET

HOW THEY WALK
Bears can stand up on 2 legs, but they walk on all fours, moving 2 legs forward on one side, and then moving 2 legs forward on the other.

THE LARGEST LAND CARNIVORE

EATING ANYTHING
Bears are included in the carnivore group, but the only one that is almost exclusively a meat-eater is the polar bear. Other bears will eat practically anything, including meat, all types of plants, fruit, insects and even honey.

MUSCLES
The largest bears are extremely strong. Their muscle strength is tremendous, especially the muscles of the neck and the upper limbs.

HEARING
The bear's ears are small and rounded. They can hear and recognize sounds from a substantial distance away. They can easily tell the difference, for example, between the footsteps of their prey and other sounds.

A LARGE AND HARD SKULL
After those of the gorilla and elephant, the bear's skull is one of the largest in the animal kingdom.

LIVER

HEART

LUNGS

BRAIN

SKULL

SHOULDER BLADE OR SCAPULA

HUMERUS

ULNA

STOMACH

SMELL
This is the bear's keenest sense. Bears are able to pick up the scent left by another animal hours later, even the scent left on a lightly touched branch.

FOREPAWS
The bear uses its paws like hands with great skill for a variety of activities: cradling young cubs, lifting a rock to look for insects or worms, picking honey from a honeycomb, fishing for trout or salmon and striking a tremendous blow to any prey.

FUR
Over the underfur, the bear has a thick coat of fur to protect it from cold in winter. The thickness and color vary according to the species.

PALMS
The palms of the paws and soles of the feet are covered with hair. This hair is insulation from the cold and it prevents the polar bear from slipping when moving over the ice.

THE GIRAFFE:

Giraffes are *ruminants* like sheep, cattle and oxen. The name ruminant comes from the word "ruminate," which means to chew a cud.

The giraffe, like all other ruminants, has a large and complex stomach consisting of four sections. When giraffes eat, they swallow grass and leaves as quickly as possible and store them in the first section of their stomach, where digestion begins. Later, the same food will return to their mouth to be chewed again. This process is called ruminating.

The advantages of a long neck.
The giraffe is the tallest animal in the world. The height of the male from head to foot can reach 20 feet (6m).

The incredible length of the neck allows giraffes to reach high branches of trees and is an extraordinary advantage in spotting danger nearby.

The life of a giraffe.
Giraffes live in herds that move slowly except when startled. Male giraffes live alone in areas with many trees, while females with their young prefer areas with less vegetation. When it is time to reproduce, the males visit the females. One year and a few months later, a young giraffe will be born—always only one, but a big one—almost 7 feet (2m) tall!

Spots.
The spots on the skin of giraffes are like our fingerprints. There are distinct types of spots according to species, but each giraffe is born with a specific design that never changes.

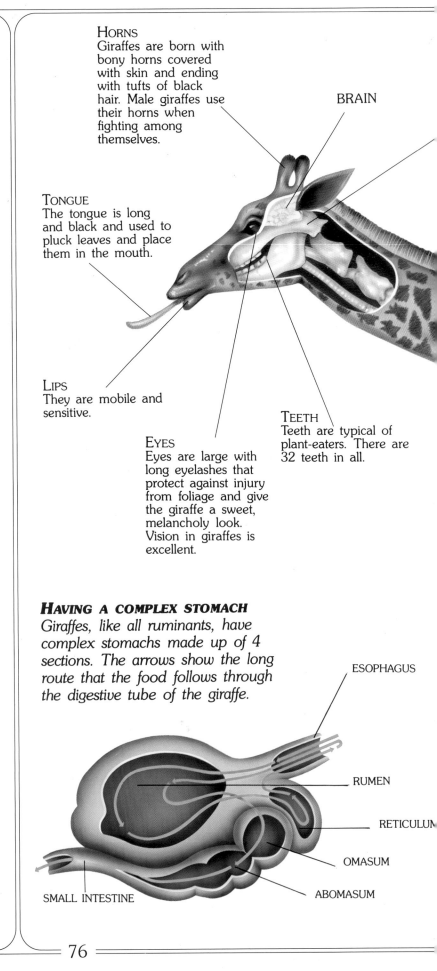

HORNS
Giraffes are born with bony horns covered with skin and ending with tufts of black hair. Male giraffes use their horns when fighting among themselves.

BRAIN

TONGUE
The tongue is long and black and used to pluck leaves and place them in the mouth.

LIPS
They are mobile and sensitive.

EYES
Eyes are large with long eyelashes that protect against injury from foliage and give the giraffe a sweet, melancholy look. Vision in giraffes is excellent.

TEETH
Teeth are typical of plant-eaters. There are 32 teeth in all.

HAVING A COMPLEX STOMACH
Giraffes, like all ruminants, have complex stomachs made up of 4 sections. The arrows show the long route that the food follows through the digestive tube of the giraffe.

ESOPHAGUS

RUMEN

RETICULUM

OMASUM

ABOMASUM

SMALL INTESTINE

THE TALLEST ANIMAL

SKULL
Around the skull, the giraffe accumulates bony material (especially males) that gives rise to 3 to 5 horns. The weight of a female's skull is often about 10 pounds (4.5kg) and that of the adult male, 33 pounds (15kg)!

A MENU OF PLANTS
Giraffes are plant-eaters. Because they do not chew meat, they don't have upper incisor teeth.

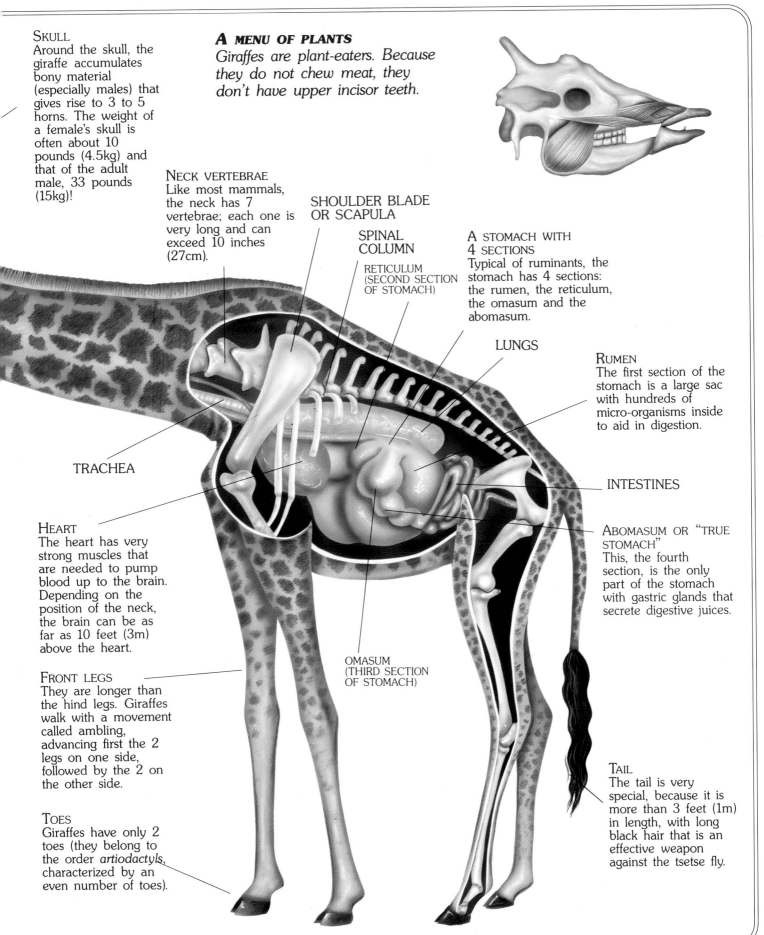

NECK VERTEBRAE
Like most mammals, the neck has 7 vertebrae; each one is very long and can exceed 10 inches (27cm).

SHOULDER BLADE OR SCAPULA

SPINAL COLUMN

RETICULUM (SECOND SECTION OF STOMACH)

A STOMACH WITH 4 SECTIONS
Typical of ruminants, the stomach has 4 sections: the rumen, the reticulum, the omasum and the abomasum.

LUNGS

RUMEN
The first section of the stomach is a large sac with hundreds of micro-organisms inside to aid in digestion.

TRACHEA

HEART
The heart has very strong muscles that are needed to pump blood up to the brain. Depending on the position of the neck, the brain can be as far as 10 feet (3m) above the heart.

INTESTINES

ABOMASUM OR "TRUE STOMACH"
This, the fourth section, is the only part of the stomach with gastric glands that secrete digestive juices.

FRONT LEGS
They are longer than the hind legs. Giraffes walk with a movement called ambling, advancing first the 2 legs on one side, followed by the 2 on the other side.

OMASUM (THIRD SECTION OF STOMACH)

TOES
Giraffes have only 2 toes (they belong to the order *artiodactyls*, characterized by an even number of toes).

TAIL
The tail is very special, because it is more than 3 feet (1m) in length, with long black hair that is an effective weapon against the tsetse fly.

There are only 2 species of camel: the one-humped African, or dromedary, camel and the two-humped Bactrian camel.

In the desert, but also in the mountains. The one-humped camel is domesticated and used by the Bedouin and Tuareg (Berber) people of North Africa and the Near East. The two-humped camel is found in the Gobi Desert of Asia and also in the Himalayan Mountains at a height of 13,000 feet (4,000m).

A hard life in the desert. Desert climate is very extreme. Temperatures reaching well over 176°F (80°C) during the day and dropping to below freezing at night are possible. In addition, there is a great scarcity of water and food. Camels have developed a number of strategies to confront the harsh conditions of desert life.

One of them is to store water in the form of a layer of fat below the hump. Others are to greatly reduce their need to drink, to sweat and to urinate. Also, camels know how to take advantage of the scarce food found in the desert.

All desert terrain. The camel's body is perfectly suited to being the best desert "vehicle." Because its feet are cushioned and spread for support, camels do not sink into the sand. They have long eyelashes to protect their eyes during sandstorms and from sun glare. Their nasal openings can seal tightly to keep sand out.

SINUS CAVITY
This is an empty space situated under the forehead. As the camel breathes in, moisture is added to the air. When the camel exhales, water from the air in the lungs is recovered.

LIPS
The upper lip is divided into two parts for easier access to food. The lower lip has a wide, hard rim for grabbing prickly stalks and leaves.

SOFT PALATE
The camel can pull this part of the palate outside of its mouth and inflate it, a sign of excitement.

PALATE

NASAL OPENINGS
Like the eyes, the nasal passages must be protected from sand. To do this, the nasal openings can close tightly.

SALIVARY GLANDS
Camels have a number of salivary glands that aid in the digestion of vegetables.

TRACHEA

ESOPHAGUS

NECK

A STOREHOUSE OF RESERVES
Obviously, camels cannot store water in their humps in liquid form. The hump actually stores fat, which can be converted to energy without using water. So, when water is scarce (almost always), camels have an extra supply of energy "on their backs."

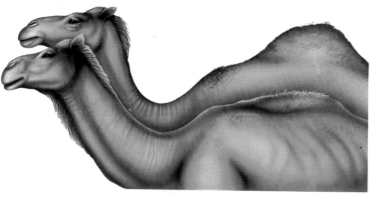

THE CAMEL: KING OF THE DESERT

EYES
Large eyelashes protect the large eyes of the camel from sun and sand.

NECK GLAND
A gland located at the back of the neck gives off an odor that is very appealing to other camels during mating. During courting, camels rub their necks together and intertwine them.

HUMP
The hump is no more than a large mass of fat that serves as a reserve of water and energy. When no water is at hand, the fat is converted into calories for energy.

SHIP OF THE DESERT
Camels are especially well equipped to transport cargo in the desert. The soles of their feet are soft, wide and adaptable to the terrain. They do not sink in the sand.

LUNG

FUR
A thick layer of fur protects the camel from high temperatures during the day and prevents heat from escaping quickly when temperatures drop at night.

HEART

RIBS

STOMACH

INTESTINE

FALSE ELBOW
The hand bones are so long that they look like another long leg bone.

SOLES OF THE FEET
The soles of the camel's feet have sacs of fat under the toenails. These sacs help to spread the weight of the animal over a wider surface and keep it from sinking in the sand.

Elephants are the largest living land animals. They belong to the order *Proboscidea*, which contains only 2 species: the African elephant and the Asian elephant.

A true glutton. Elephants are vegetarians, which means they eat only plants, but they need to eat up to 440 pounds (200kg) per day. They use their trunks to pull up plants and pick leaves from trees and their tusks to strip bark from trees. Elephants also need a lot of water, about 26 gallons (100l) per day. They use their tusks to search for water by digging in dry riverbeds.

When they bathe in rivers, they shower themselves by throwing water with their trunks. They also like frequent mud baths to keep their skin free of flies and other insects.

An elephant is born. The mother elephant has the longest pregnancy of any animal—almost 2 years! It is not surprising then that the newborn is one of the largest babies in the world, measuring about 3 feet (1m) high and weighing about 265 pounds (120kg).

The baby elephant suckles until it is almost 2 years old. From that age on, growth is very rapid. At 6 years, an elephant already weighs 2,200 pounds (1,000kg).

A "weighty" animal. The African elephant, the largest land animal, can weigh more than 6 tons (6,000kg), almost as much as 100 people.

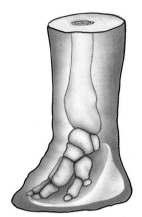

A LIGHT STEP
Despite their strong, heavy feet, elephants walk practically "on tiptoe." Its toes are protected by a thick cushion of fat that covers the soles of their feet and heels.

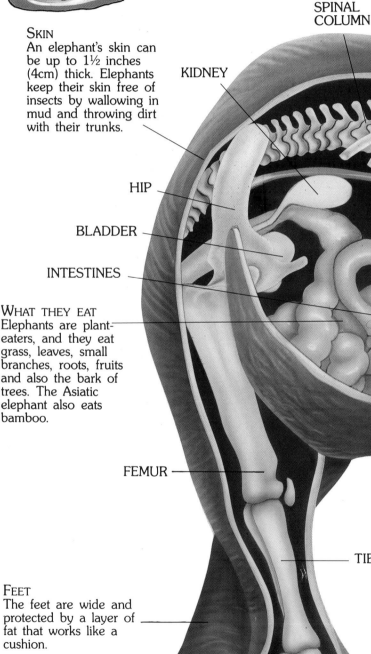

SKIN
An elephant's skin can be up to 1½ inches (4cm) thick. Elephants keep their skin free of insects by wallowing in mud and throwing dirt with their trunks.

SPINAL COLUMN

KIDNEY

HIP

BLADDER

INTESTINES

WHAT THEY EAT
Elephants are plant-eaters, and they eat grass, leaves, small branches, roots, fruits and also the bark of trees. The Asiatic elephant also eats bamboo.

FEMUR

TIBIA

FEET
The feet are wide and protected by a layer of fat that works like a cushion.

THE ENORMOUS ELEPHANT

EARS
The elephant's large ears have well-developed hearing organs that allow it to hear the bleats or cries of other elephants several miles away.

SHOULDER BLADE

STOMACH

VISION
The elephant does not have good vision. Its eyes are small and can see only a short distance.

BRAIN
The elephant has a large, strong cranium and a very developed brain. The elephant's brain is larger than that of other land mammals, including humans.

TEETH
An elephant has only 6 teeth at a time. When a tooth wears away and falls out, a new one grows in. During an elephant's lifetime of about 60 years, 4 groups of teeth are lost. After the last group wears out, the elephant can no longer chew, and dies.

TUSKS
Tusks are incisor teeth of the upper jaw. They grow during all of an elephant's life, but they never get too long because they wear away with use.

ESOPHAGUS

TRACHEA

LUNGS

HEART

HUMERUS

NOSE AND "HAND"
The trunk is a muscular extension of the nose and upper lip. It has many uses. Among other things, it is used to pick leaves and fruit from trees. At the end of the trunk, there are several projections, called lobes, that work like the fingers of a hand.

LIVER

ULNA

SMELLING AND BREATHING
At the end of the trunk, there are nasal openings. Smell is very important in relationships among elephants, since it is by scent that they know if they belong to the same herd. Elephants can also breathe through the trunk while submerging their bodies in water and wading through a river.

— CUSHION OF FAT

THE KANGAROO:

Kangaroos live only in Australia. Because this continent is surrounded by water and has been isolated from other land areas since the Tertiary Period, many of its animals have evolved differently from those in the rest of the world.

Kangaroos are marsupials. The distinguishing feature of marsupials is that many females have a pouch in the abdomen, called a marsupium, where the mammary glands are located and the young finish their development.

A fantastic voyage. Small kangaroos spend the first months of their lives in the marsupium. How do they get there after they are born?

At birth, a young kangaroo is very small, weighing only a fraction of an ounce. It is hairless and has undeveloped eyes and ears.

Led by smell, the newborns begin their climb by holding onto the skin of the mother's abdomen. After about five minutes of effort, they reach the edge of the pouch, crawl inside and begin to suckle.

The young kangaroo will not run loose until it is ready to leave the marsupium in about 6 months.

Olympic jumps. The longest kangaroo jumps have measured over 36 feet (11m) in length, much more than those of an Olympic athlete!

A giant Australian. The grey kangaroo is the largest species and can measure up to 11 feet (3.3m) from its nose to the tip of its tail.

CHAMPION JUMPER
The kangaroo runs on large hind legs that, in combination with its feet, work like springs. It folds its front legs under its chest and uses them only for balance. The tail acts like a balancing pole.

WOMB
Kangaroos reproduce rapidly. The female may have a baby in her pouch and another in her womb at the same time.

TAIL
The tail is long—from 26 inches (65cm) to 3½ feet (105cm)— strong and muscular. It helps to support the kangaroo when it is standing up and gives increased balance when the kangaroo jumps.

BONES OF THE TAIL

ANIMAL WITH A POUCH

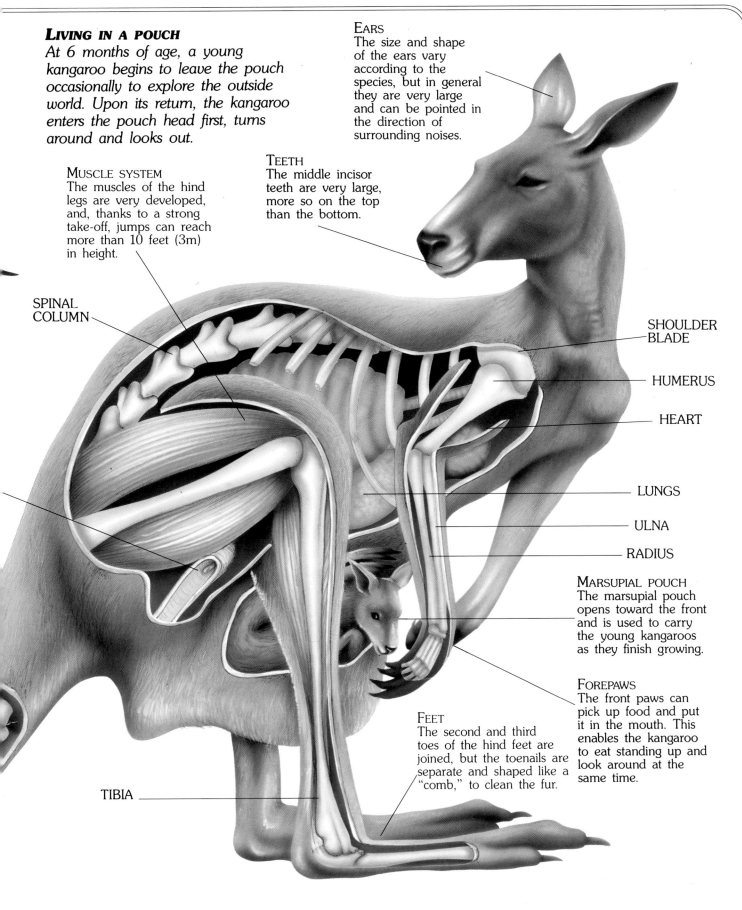

LIVING IN A POUCH

At 6 months of age, a young kangaroo begins to leave the pouch occasionally to explore the outside world. Upon its return, the kangaroo enters the pouch head first, turns around and looks out.

MUSCLE SYSTEM
The muscles of the hind legs are very developed, and, thanks to a strong take-off, jumps can reach more than 10 feet (3m) in height.

SPINAL COLUMN

EARS
The size and shape of the ears vary according to the species, but in general they are very large and can be pointed in the direction of surrounding noises.

TEETH
The middle incisor teeth are very large, more so on the top than the bottom.

SHOULDER BLADE

HUMERUS

HEART

LUNGS

ULNA

RADIUS

MARSUPIAL POUCH
The marsupial pouch opens toward the front and is used to carry the young kangaroos as they finish growing.

FOREPAWS
The front paws can pick up food and put it in the mouth. This enables the kangaroo to eat standing up and look around at the same time.

FEET
The second and third toes of the hind feet are joined, but the toenails are separate and shaped like a "comb," to clean the fur.

TIBIA

THE DOLPHIN:

Like humans, dolphins are mammals, but they have made many anatomical changes to adapt to life in water. We find them on the high seas, along the coasts and in large river systems. They usually swim in groups, or schools.

The dolphin's sonar. Light does not travel well underwater, so seeing is difficult and colors are hard to detect. For marine animals like dolphins, which need to move quickly to hunt, not being able to distinguish prey or enemies at a distance is a tremendous problem. Dolphins have solved it through the use of sound. Their method is called echolocation and it is very similar to the radar used by bats.

When there is nothing unusual nearby, dolphins emit a continual signal that gives information about the area, the location of the shore, depth of water, and so on. When a new echo is received, a dolphin must first get more information: At what distance is the object? In which direction? Is it a shark?

To do this, it will send out a series of very rapid clicks whose echoes will tell about the object or prey.

More teeth than anyone. Some dolphins hold the record among mammals for numbers of teeth. They can have up to 250!

Sleeping very little. Normally, dolphins sleep only 2 or 3 hours per day, but sometimes they sleep so soundly that, while floating on the surface, they crash into ships.

SOUND EMITTED

SOUND BOUNCED BACK (ECHO)

How a dolphin's sonar works
When dolphins detect prey nearby, they emit very rapid clicks, searching for more information. The sound of the click bounces off the object, produces an echo and returns to the dolphin, whose brain interprets the information.

KIDNEYS

INTESTINE

RIBS
The ribs of dolphins are somewhat delicate and not strongly joined to the breastbone or the spinal column. For this reason, the thorax cannot easily support the dolphin's weight if it runs aground and outside of water.

FLUKE (TAIL FIN)
Placed horizontally, the fluke moves up and down. Because of its powerful thrust, dolphins can jump high and achieve great speeds.

SKIN
The dolphin's smooth, hairless skin allows for rapid swimming, since it offers less resistance to the water. The skin must always be kept wet, even when a dolphin is moved from one aquarium to another.

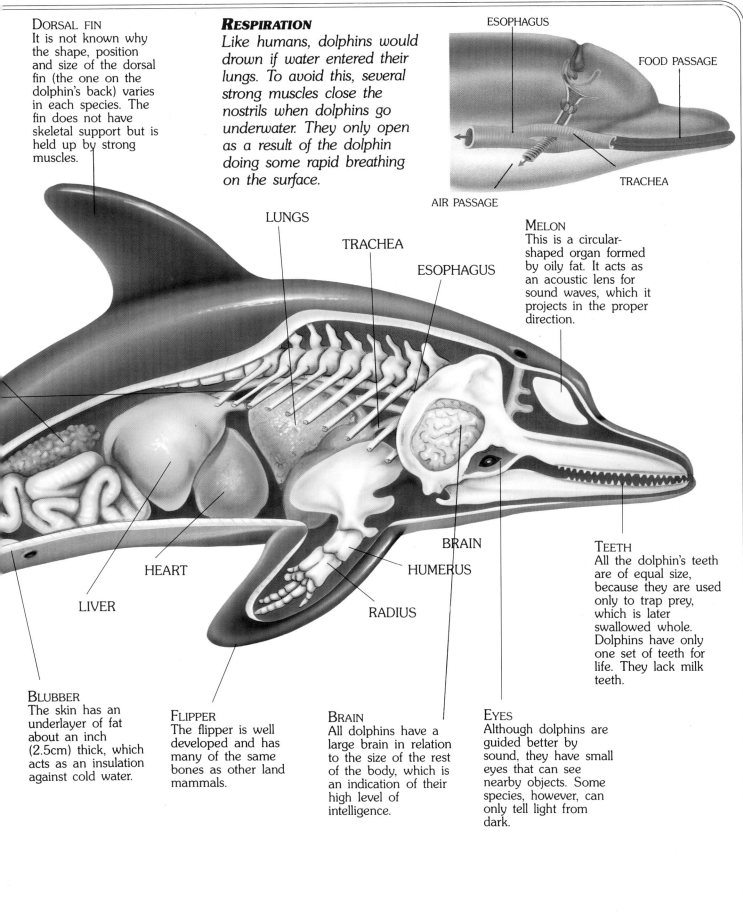

DORSAL FIN
It is not known why the shape, position and size of the dorsal fin (the one on the dolphin's back) varies in each species. The fin does not have skeletal support but is held up by strong muscles.

RESPIRATION
Like humans, dolphins would drown if water entered their lungs. To avoid this, several strong muscles close the nostrils when dolphins go underwater. They only open as a result of the dolphin doing some rapid breathing on the surface.

ESOPHAGUS

FOOD PASSAGE

AIR PASSAGE

TRACHEA

LUNGS

TRACHEA

ESOPHAGUS

MELON
This is a circular-shaped organ formed by oily fat. It acts as an acoustic lens for sound waves, which it projects in the proper direction.

BRAIN

HUMERUS

HEART

LIVER

RADIUS

TEETH
All the dolphin's teeth are of equal size, because they are used only to trap prey, which is later swallowed whole. Dolphins have only one set of teeth for life. They lack milk teeth.

BLUBBER
The skin has an underlayer of fat about an inch (2.5cm) thick, which acts as an insulation against cold water.

FLIPPER
The flipper is well developed and has many of the same bones as other land mammals.

BRAIN
All dolphins have a large brain in relation to the size of the rest of the body, which is an indication of their high level of intelligence.

EYES
Although dolphins are guided better by sound, they have small eyes that can see nearby objects. Some species, however, can only tell light from dark.

Although whales live in the sea, they are mammals just as dolphins and humans are. They belong to the order *Cetacea*, which has 2 suborders: cetaceans with teeth, or Odontoceti, such as dolphins and killer whales; and the cetaceans without teeth, or Mysticeti, the group that includes this baleen whale.

Living in water. Whales breathe through blow-holes situated in the top of the head. They breathe when they raise their heads above water. When the whale submerges, water pressure closes the blow-hole and prevents water from entering. When the whale reaches the surface again, the blow-hole opens . As air leaves the lungs of the whale, a spout of water vapor is released that can shoot upwards as high as 65 feet (20m)

How they swim. Whales swim by moving their fluke (tail fin). Unlike the vertical tail fins of fish, the whale's fin is horizontal. The whale moves it up and down, striking the water. Fins on both sides of the body are used to change direction and to prevent the whale from turning over while swimming.

Giant of the sea. There are several families of baleen whale. Among them are the rorquals, which include the blue whale, the largest animal in the world. It measures up to 100 feet (30m) and can weigh as much as 143 tons (130,000kg), the weight of almost 20 elephants!

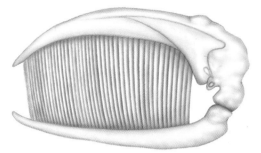

A MONSTROUS FILTER
The baleen whale filters plankton through 200 to 400 fringed plates, or baleen, situated between its upper and lower jaws. These are arranged like pages in a book.

BLOW-HOLE
A series of ducts and valves opens and closes to keep water from getting into the blow-hole of the whale.

TAIL
This is shaped by strongly intertwined muscles and tendons that lend rigidity. In some species, the tail measures 15 feet (4.5m) across.

DORSAL FIN
Although missing in some species, whales usually have a dorsal fin in the middle of their back or slightly farther back. It has no bones in it—just strong fibrous tissue.

KIDNEYS

TESTICLES

BLUBBER
The enormous layer of fat underneath the skin helps to maintain the whale's body temperature even in sub-freezing waters.

ROLLED-UP PENIS

THE WHALE: THE LARGEST ANIMAL

TONGUE
The tongue can weigh 4½ tons (4,082kg). Pushed upward against the roof of the mouth, it expels the water that has entered the mouth. It then sucks the baleen that trap filtered organisms.

UPPER JAW
The upper jaw is very large and supports hundreds of baleen.

BALEEN
On either side of the upper jaw, there are between 200 and 400 baleen, rough plates with long filaments that filter and hold the small organisms on which the animal feeds.

EYES
The eyes are mobile and well adapted to life in the ocean. At great depths, the pupils grow wide to catch the scant amount of light.

BRAIN

LUNGS

SPINAL COLUMN

THROAT PLEATS
In rorqual whales, the throat has a series of pleats that can be dilated. This allows the whale to gulp down enormous quantities of water to get sufficient food.

VERY RAPID DEVELOPMENT
During pregnancy, the fetus increases considerably in size and weight. In the last 2 months, it can gain 4,400 pounds (2,000kg). The drawing shows the fetus of a blue whale.

HEART

LIVER

RIBS

STOMACH

INTESTINE
Depending upon the species, the intestine can be very long to aid in digesting an enormous quantity of food—up to 3½ tons (3,175kg) daily.

FLIPPER
Although the sizes are very different, the bones of the flipper are the same as the arm bones in humans, but they are only movable in the shoulder joint.

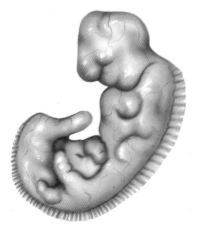

The dinosaurs

Some 215 million years ago, the first dinosaurs, descendants of a group of reptiles, began their conquest of the earth, which they dominated for more than 150 million years. Dinosaurs came in a large variety of shapes and sizes, from predators on two legs, like Gallimimus and Composagnathus, to large plant-eaters, like Diplodocus and Brachiosaurus. But the one we hear the most about is Tyrannosaurus rex, the largest meat-eater that ever existed.

Dinosaurs were a group of large *reptiles* that dominated the earth between 230 and 65 million years ago. The word dinosaur means "terrible lizard."

Two groups of dinosaurs.
Paleontologists divide dinosaurs into 2 groups, depending upon their skeletal structure: "bird hipped," which had the pubis bone pointing toward the front; and "reptile hipped," which had it pointing toward the rear.

A voracious appetite.
The largest dinosaurs were the most non-threatening because they were plant-eaters. Brachiosaurus, for example, was as tall as a three-story building and weighed as much as three elephants, but it ate only plants. It probably needed more than 3,307 pounds (1,500kg) of food daily.

Tyrannosaurus rex.
The largest meat-eating animal that ever lived was Tyrannosaurus rex, which you see illustrated here.

Tyrannosaurus rex was as long as 8 people stretched end to end. It surpassed a giraffe in height and weighed more than an adult elephant.

His teeth were large and curved inward, so that it was difficult for other animals to escape. Moreover, one butt from his head could finish off many a dinosaur who dared to argue over food.

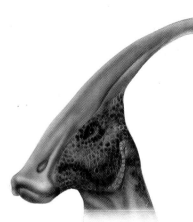

A PROTECTIVE SHIELD
The crest of this Triceratops could stop blows. Its main function, however, may have been in displays to members of its own species.

A LOUDSPEAKER ON THE HEAD
Parasaurolophus had a hollow tube on its head that acted as a loudspeaker. This may have been used to sound an alarm or scare off an enemy.

LEGS
Tyrannosaurus rex could do more than 18 miles (30km) per hour—faster than a person in full run—in spite of its 8-ton (7,258kg) weight, for short-distance sprints.

SKIN
The skin of dinosaurs was probably made up of scales, like present-day reptiles Their skin color is not known.

TAIL VERTEBRAE

TAIL
The muscular tail was used for balance while running or attacking. By using the tail for balance, one Tyrannosaurus rex could stand up and measure its prowess against another!

FEET
Tyrannosaurus rex walked on tiptoe, using 3 long toes ending in claws. He would have left footprints the size of the wheel of a car.

THE PREHISTORIC DINOSAURS

RIBS
The ribs of Tyrannosaurus rex were very strong. Otherwise, organs like its heart and lungs could have been crushed when it lay down to rest.

ARMS
Arms were small and unable even to reach the mouth. Each hand had only 2 fingers ending in claws; some believe they were used to hold the prey while eating.

TEETH
Each of the ferocious teeth measured 7 inches (18cm) in length, longer than a pen. Curved and sharp as a knife, they could cleanly cut through bone. If broken or worn away, they would be replaced.

SKULL
The skull had to be very hard to withstand the blows received when fighting and violently attacking and eating prey. At the same time, it was also light, with many empty spaces.

EYES
Like most predators, Tyrannosaurus rex had good vision.

HIP
Examples of the two groups of dinosaurs divided according to hip position are Tyrannosaurus rex, which had a "reptile-type" hip, and Triceratops, which had a "bird-type" hip.

TRACHEA

ESOPHAGUS

TONGUE
Tyrannosaurus rex had a tongue as large as the arm of an adult human. Big chunks of meat torn from victims with one swift shake of the head could be swallowed with the help of this muscular tongue.

PUBIS

HEART

LIVER

LUNG

INTESTINE

SPINAL COLUMN

STOMACH

DINOSAUR EGGS
Like other reptiles but unlike amphibians, dinosaurs probably laid eggs on land, not in water. The young developed inside the egg with the tail wrapped around the body.

TYRANNOSAURUS REX

Abdomen. The rear part of the body. The abdomen typically contains the intestines and reproductive organs.

Ammonia Ions. Dissolved molecules of ammonia, a compound that contains nitrogen.

Amphibians. Four-legged animals that live in the water during the larval stage, and usually live on land as adults. This group includes frogs and salamanders.

Antennae. Long, movable sense organs that project from the head of insects and some other animals.

Aorta. A large blood vessel that carries blood away from the heart and towards other parts of the body.

Arachnids. A group of animals that includes spiders, scorpions, mites, and ticks.

Atrial Cavity. The cavity inside a sponge where the sponge extracts food particles and releases wastes into the water.

Bivalves. A group of animals that have a two-part shell. This group includes clams.

Cephalopods. A group of marine animals that have arms (and often tentacles) surrounding the mouth. This group includes octopus and squid.

Cetaceans. A group of marine mammals that includes whales and dolphins.

Chondrichthyes. Cartilaginous fish.

Cloaca. A chamber at the end of the digestive tract that receives wastes and ducts from the reproductive organs. It is used in mating in many animals.

Coelenterates. A group of marine animals that look like plants. This group includes jellyfish and sea anemones.

Crustaceans. A group of mostly aquatic animals that have a hard shell and two pairs of antennae. This group includes lobsters and crabs.

Diffraction. The phenomenon of light or sound waves being bent when passing through objects.

Esophagus. A muscular tube that connects the mouth with the stomach.

Femur. The thigh or upper leg, often referring to the long bone found in the thigh.

Fertilization. The union of sperm and egg to form a new individual.

Fibula. One of two bones in the lower leg. The other bone is called the *tibia*.

Gastric Cavity. Stomach cavity.

Gonads. Reproductive organs. The male gonads are called *testes*; the female gonads are called *ovaries*.

Hepatopancreas. An organ that acts like both a liver and a pancreas; it stores nutrients, and makes digestive juices and important hormones.

Humerus. The upper arm, often referring to the long bone found in the upper arm.

Hymenoptera. A group of insects that includes ants and bees.

Intestine. A muscular tube connecting the stomach and anus. Nutrients are absorbed from digested food in the intestine.

Keel. A raised ridge on the breastbone that provides a place for large muscles to attach.

Kidney. An organ that removes wastes from the blood. These wastes are concentrated in urine, which can then be eliminated from the body.

Larvae. An early stage of development of some animals. Larvae don't look like adults; they reach their adult stage later, after they have grown larger.

Lepidoptera. The group of insects that contains butterflies and moths.

Ligaments. Bands of elastic tissue that connect hard parts of the skeleton.

Mandibles. The jaws of an animal.

Manubrium. The central part of the body of a jellyfish. It contains most of the digestive system.

Maxillary Glands. Glands found in the mouth region. They produce saliva, which helps begin the digestion of food.

Mollusks. Soft-bodied animals protected by a hard shell.

Nictitating Membrane. A transparent inner eyelid present in some mammals and amphibians.

Ovary. The organ that makes eggs in female animals.

Ovule. Another name for the egg produced by female animals.

Palate. The roof of the mouth.

Pallial Cavity. The cavity that contains the internal organs.

Parasite. An animal that lives inside or on the body of another animal of a different species, on which it feeds.

Pen. The rodlike internal skeleton of a squid.

Pharynx. The throat cavity.

Plankton. Microscopic animals and plants that make up the diet of many marine animals.

Polyp. A roughly ball-shaped structure that grows on a stalk. It contains units designed for either feeding or reproduction.

Predator. An animal that obtains food by killing and eating other animals.

Glossary/Index

Proboscis. A muscular tube that extends from the head of an animal. The proboscis is used either for feeding or breathing, depending on the animal.

Projectile. Something that can be extended with great speed. The projectile tongue of some lizards moves so fast that a human can't see it.

Radials. Canals that are part of the digestive system of a jellyfish. Digested food is distributed to the body of the jellyfish through these canals.

Radius. One of the two bones in the forearm (the other bone is called the *ulna*).

Regurgitate. To cough up partially digested food into the mouth. This food can then be rechewed and swallowed, or it may be fed to the animal's young.

Rodents. A group of mammals whose teeth are specialized for gnawing. This group contains rats, mice, squirrels and beavers.

Rostrum. The front end of the snout of an animal. The rostrum often extends forward above the front teeth.

Ruminants. A group of plant-eating mammals that has a complex stomach that uses bacteria to help digest grass and other tough plant material.

Savannah. A great expanse of grassland that is generally flat and has only a few scattered trees.

Siphon. A muscular tube that extends out of the body of some marine animals. The animals move by forcing water out of the siphon under pressure.

Spawn. To deposit eggs.

Spermatozoid. Sperm; the reproductive cells of male animals.

Testes. The organ that makes sperm in male animals.

Thorax. The front part of the body. The thorax usually contains the heart and lungs.

Tibia. One of two bones in the lower leg. The other bone is called the fibula.

Trachea. Reinforced tubes that connect the lungs with the throat. Air passes through the nose and mouth into the throat, through the trachea, and into the lungs.

Ulna. One of the two bones in the forearm (the other bone is called the *radius*).

Urostyle. A bone composed of several fused tail vertebrae.

Vertebrae. The bones that make up the backbone.